Book Stack and Shelving for Libraries

BOOK STACK AND SHELVING FOR LIBRARIES

DESIGNED BY BERNARD R. GREEN, C. E.

THE SNEAD AND COMPANY
IRON WORKS
JERSEY CITY, N. J.

~~No. 3800~~ withdrawn v-55

U S PATENTS

No 436,704
No 466,033
No 516,734
No 520,191
No 11,401 — Re-i-sue
No 565,189
No 774,984
No 776,233
No 791,153
No 791,154
No 791,155
No 791,156
No 798,430
No 798,431
No 798,432

N
Sn 2
1908

Copyright, 1908, by
THE SNEAD AND COMPANY IRON WORKS
Jersey City, N J

16948B

BOOK STACK AND SHELVING FOR LIBRARIES

Requisites of a Library Book Stack.

Every active library containing any considerable number of volumes requires an arrangement of shelving embodying all of the following features, namely

1 Accommodation for books of every variety, size and kind of binding
2 Shelves easily and quickly adjustable and interchangeable by any library attendant and readily and compactly stowed away close at hand when temporarily displaced.
3 Permitting every desirable classification, arrangement and rearrangement of the books at will
4 Affording free and instant access to any volume at any time
5 Having not only certain main corridors, stairs and lifts for direct access to the books and for free communication both laterally and vertically throughout the stack in its several tiers, but readily yielding additional passages anywhere
6 Proper supports for books on partially filled shelves
7 Maximum capacity and capability of indefinite extension
8 All surfaces permanently smooth and rounded to prevent injury to books or papers and protected from corrosion
9 Fireproof throughout
10 Thoroughly and safely illuminated by day and by night
11 Naturally clean and readily kept free from accumulated dust
12 Furnishing no lodgment or comfort to book pests
13 Immunity from injury from leaky roof or ceiling
14 Even temperature and ventilation not only throughout the stack in general but through the individual shelves and their supports, so that practically the only obstruction to free circulation of air and light is offered by the books themselves
15. Free, easy and direct communication at will in any direction throughout the stack for the convenience of attendants
16. Convenience for all sorts of appropriate work everywhere in the stack, including direct access to books by readers when desirable as in the "open shelf" room, and the placing at convenient points of desks, cabinets, etc.
17 The fewest separate parts or pieces and the simplest construction consistent with strength and rigidity
18 Location in close communication with reading, cataloguing and delivery rooms.

THE SNEAD AND COMPANY IRON WORKS

ORIGINAL DESIGN   Until the construction of the great building for the Library of Congress was taken in hand for the shelving of millions of volumes of books, and the then rapidly increasing variety and bulk of library collections of all kinds, no system of shelving on a large, complete and thoroughly economical scale had been devised   Some small stacks had been built of combinations of iron and wood, but all were ill ventilated, very unequally warmed, dusty, close and overheated in their upper parts, inconvenient of access and poorly lighted

Librarians were correspondingly dissatisfied and unhappy and the theory of shelving on the stack principle was consequently disapproved, and other schemes of single or of few tiers, with alcoves, etc , were attempted but found prohibitive in distances between parts, extent of administration, size of building and grounds, and therefore of cost of construction and maintenance

Of the eighteen requisites of a complete and satisfactory stack system of shelving above enumerated, scarcely one was to be found in any existing library

The problem was consequently new in almost all its elements. To solve it the needs of library administration were carefully studied and the results finally embodied in the system of shelving and stack construction which the Library of Congress, Washington, D C , now contains and which has met the unqualified approval of all librarians

It is this system of shelving devised by Mr Green, the engineer in charge, which, with modifications and improvements up to date, adapting it to all modern requirements of libraries, large or small, public or private, is herein described and illustrated, as manufactured by THE SNEAD & CO IRON WORKS

As stated, this system was the original design, on a comprehensive scale, of modern shelving for libraries   All other systems competing with it are makeshifts based on it but modified in minor details for the purpose of avoiding the patents and gaining the market

None of them is an improvement, and all are, on the whole, inferior, because to reduce cost, certain details of the complete original have been omitted

HISTORY   The original of the modern metallic book stack was designed for the extension of Gore Hall, the Library of Harvard College, at Cambridge, Mass , in 1875

It consisted of cast iron open work partitions or shelf supports and deck

BOOK STACK AND SHELVING FOR LIBRARIES

framing, with cast iron perforated decks, and wooden shelves. This stack was copied in an extension of the Athenæum Library, Boston, and for that of the Army Medical Library, in Washington.

It was a distinct advance in compact permanent shelving in its day, but contained the comparative conditions of the architectural foundry work of the time. No other important advance had been made in economical, permanent, book shelving before the construction of the Library of Congress, begun in 1889, when the problem of the relatively mammoth stacks was presented. It was solved by Mr Green, the superintendent of the construction, by the design and inventions which were carried out as the stacks now stand in the building, after an exhaustive consideration of the needs of libraries and the available new materials and resources of the foundry and architectural iron manufacture at that time. The ground was so completely covered that few material improvements in methods, materials, or cost, have since been made, although many manufacturers have undertaken it, in competition with the Green stack in the market, and great numbers of stacks have been built throughout this and other countries. The natural cause of this is the extreme simplicity of parts and the minimum of quantity and space occupied by the materials of construction attained, leaving the maximum of bulk available for the books and reducing the cost to the lowest terms.

The original stacks in the Library of Congress, three in number, nine tiers in height, containing forty-three miles of shelves with capacity for 2,000,000 volumes, have been in constant and very active use for ten years without a hitch or complaint of any kind. Not a shelf or other part of the great combination has given trouble, nor has any repair, however trifling, been needed and the whole is as perfect and serviceable as at the beginning.

These stacks have therefore naturally been the standard towards which all designs have been aimed from the start, and they have never been outclassed in any particular. This is not merely the judgment of the interested manufacturers but the disinterested opinion of all who have really learned and understood the subject.

Since the original stacks were built, the manufacturers, THE SNEAD & CO IRON WORKS, have introduced the several perfections in iron casting, connections, and beautiful workmanship that have been acquired in their manufacturing arts, so that their stacks of the present day contain material improvements.

THE SNEAD AND COMPANY IRON WORKS

<small>Arrangement</small>

GENERAL PRINCIPLES Books are most advantageously shelved in double-faced parallel ranges Radial ranges waste space Glass or illuminating tile decks will serve to transmit strong sky light down through one or two tiers, but not more In lofty stacks, therefore, side lights are indispensable and must be amply provided where daylight is to be depended on.

<small>High Stacks Must Have Side Light</small>

<small>Materials Fireproof</small>

All parts should be of fireproof material

<small>Requirements for Shelves</small>

Shelves about 9 inches wide, 3 feet long, thin as possible for strength and stiffness, uniform size and interchangeable, open work and light, quickly adjustable, but firm and practically immovable when in place, perfectly flat without flanges or projections, perfectly smooth all over, and free from sharp points or edges, durable and permanently safe from corrosion or injurious coatings

<small>Construction Uniform Throughout</small>

Stack tiers uniform with and superimposed on each other, for greatest economy of space, interchangeability and convenience, besides best lighting and least expensive construction

<small>Tiers Seven Feet High</small>

Tiers about 7 feet from deck surface to deck surface

<small>Shelf Supports Compact</small>

Partitions or shelf supports thin as possible, in open work and perfectly straight, flat, and rigid

<small>Flooring Marble or Glass</small>

Decks of solid material—preferably white marble, next glass, partly for translucency These give quiet decks

Aisle decks solid from side to side

<small>Deck Slits</small>

Range decks,—those between the shelf ranges—solid through the middle with a longitudinal slit or opening 5 inches wide along each side for light, ventilation, oral communication, safety of lower shelf books from injury by cleaning decks, moving trucks, etc, through between the ranges, and for saving in first cost of deck material

<small>Curb Angle</small>

Slits in decks protected by half-inch curb from articles or litter on deck being pushed off.

<small>Electric Lighting Best</small>

Day lighting irregular, unsatisfactory and often uneconomical. Tolerable for small stacks or cases of shelving

Night use generally required making it indispensable to provide ample artificial lighting system This often needed even in shelving used only in day time because of days darkened by clouds and short days of winter season in our latitude

Electric lighting at hand, perfectly safe and of moderate expense, if turned on in the shelving only where and while actually needed

BOOK STACK AND SHELVING FOR LIBRARIES

The stack should be as nearly as possible a *stack of books*, with the least possible actual material of construction visible after the books are in place

Therefore, of thin material and open work for ventilating, easy reach for dusting, poor lodgment for insects, communication between attendants, least boxed in and close, and most cheerful and airy for the attendants, fewest separate parts or pieces in construction, exposed surfaces white for reflection of light, shelves adjustable, to accommodate all kinds and sizes of books, ample artificial light under easy control   Maximum simplicity and minimum cost

Quick intercommunication between parts and decks of stack, and with reading, catalogue rooms, etc , by means of stairs, elevators, mechanical carriers, telephones, etc

CONSTRUCTION OF THE BOOK STACK   As shown in figures 1, 2 and 3, (pages 23-24-25) the shelving is placed in parallel double ranges, at right angles to the walls, which admit both the daylight and electric light directly into the passages between the ranges   The ranges rise, tier on tier, to any desired height, at intervals of seven feet from deck to deck   This is the most convenient average height for reading the titles and handling the books on the top shelf

The shelf is of uniform size throughout the stack, and adjustable to any height Its length and width may be made to suit the preference of librarians, three feet being the standard length, and eight or ten inches the width

The double book range is therefore two shelves, or sixteen to twenty inches wide   The passage between the ranges should be from three to three and a half feet, and the total center to center interval of ranges is therefore from four feet four inches to five feet two inches

All tiers may thus be precisely alike in every detail, and the shelves adjustable and interchangeable throughout the stack

The construction consists simply of cast iron skeleton shelf supports or uprights, spaced the shelf-length apart, resting on the foundation and extending from deck to deck to the top of the stack   These partitions are steadied by attachment at top and bottom to the deck bars, which are the supports of the decks

The deck bars are of steel bolted to the uprights at each deck level, and connecting the rows of uprights   The latter are also connected to each other at the deck levels by flanged bars at right angles to the deck bars   All are connected continuously through the stack, both laterally and longitudinally, from wall to wall, into

THE SNEAD AND COMPANY IRON WORKS

which they are anchored, thus bracing the uprights at every story and preventing buckling in the lower stories from the weight of books and decks above

The covering of the decks may be thin slabs of any fireproof material, preferably white marble, rubbed above and polished underneath to reflect light This covering is solid—without perforations or gratings—to prevent dust and litter from sifting through, but an open slit about five inches wide is left along each front of each book range for ventilation and light, and for conversation and the handing through, between decks, of books, papers, or other articles This open space is of great value as a protection to the books on the bottom shelf from injury by the cleaning of decks, while it also saves expense in construction of the decks

A low flange is raised on the deck bar along this slit to prevent anything lying on the deck from being pushed off

A sheet-steel diaphragm is placed in each range at each deck level to prevent dust from one story sifting down to the next, to prevent fire from running up, and to serve as a stepping plate for persons passing through any range from side to side when shelves are removed, and to avoid, when desirable, going around the range It is also a stiffening web to the construction and serves as the bottom book shelf

LIGHTING When the stack has side windows, each window may consist of a single pane of polished plate glass as wide as the passage between ranges, and nearly or quite the full height of the story or tier, permanently set air-tight into the opening at the head of each passage Those exposed to direct sunlight may be provided with blinds of translucent glass or other material, such as brass wire gauze, operated in gangs from one or several points The exterior surface of the window glass may be washed from skeleton galleries permanently provided on the walls, from a hanging seat which can be raised or lowered, or by a stream from a hose

The artificial lighting should be by electricity only, with incandescent lamps These may be of the "door-knob" or other pattern, snugly placed in the deck ceilings out of harm's way, diffusing the light throughout each range or corridor

SHELF SUPPORTS AND SHELVES The shelf partition or support is provided with a continuous row of blunt teeth on the front edge, and a corresponding row of horns or hooks on each side at the back to carry the shelves, which in turn are provided with lugs on their front corners and claw notches near

BOOK STACK AND SHELVING FOR LIBRARIES

their back corners This arrangement permits quick adjustment of shelves throughout the entire height of the tier, and also the placing of opposite shelves of the same range at any one level, making a through shelf of double width, also the placing of shelves close together if desired to receive a large volume or two lying flat

There are no loose or movable pins, brackets, screws or other parts whatever The standing partition and the movable shelf comprise the whole outfit At any point, the shelves, which are perfectly flat, like thin boards, may be removed and piled away at the top of the range, and leave all the space between the supports free for passage to and fro through the stack, or for any other purpose, such as the introduction of cabinets, etc

The shelf itself is preferably an open grating of parallel bars of steel, the top surfaces being about one-half inch wide, spaced about one-quarter of an inch apart in the clear, and perfectly smooth These are connected across at the ends by a bar containing the lugs and claw notches for support, and they are also "bridged" at one or two intervals between the ends by a small rod, as shown in figure 6, page 29 The shelf is the most complete and perfect made, or ever likely to be made It is illustrated and described on pages 48 and 49

All parts of the shelf and partition, with which books may come in contact, are perfectly smooth all over and have a hard coating that will not wear off or injure the bindings of the books

It is evident that a shelf may be made of sheet metal or wood, even of slate or glass if desired, that will take the place of the iron bar shelf here described, by simply providing the claw notch and the metal lugs on the front corners The somewhat less expensive wooden shelf may therefore be used in this system of shelving as well as in any other, and may even be made with parallel longitudinal slits if desired, so as to possess many of the merits of the metal shelf, including the attachment for the same book support used on the steel bar shelf

BOOK SUPPORTS Taking advantage of the longitudinal spaces between the parallel bars of the shelf, a locking toggle, passing between and hooking under the bars, is placed on the foot flange of a vertical metallic plate, which, while movable up to the last book on the end of the shelf, automatically locks itself in position against the books This device is shown in figure 7, page 29

THE SNEAD AND COMPANY IRON WORKS

It is extremely simple, durable and inexpensive, and yet the most convenient and reliable book support yet devised

It has no loose or separate parts, may be used anywhere in the shelving, and may be instantly removed and stowed away when not needed. It goes equally well on top of the shelf, or, inverted, in position, on the bottom of the shelf for the support of books on the shelf below. This is particularly advantageous with tall books, by holding against their tops

This support is as readily applicable to a solid shelf, either of wood or metal, if a slit be made three or four inches from the front edge to receive the toggle.

LABEL HOLDERS Also utilizing the construction of the shelf a metal label holder is made to clamp over the first two bars at front of shelf, being entirely independent of the weight of books for holding in place See figure 22, page 49

ELEVATOR AND STAIRS The stack may be provided with stairways, and with an elevator capable of lifting one or more persons with a truck load of books, and of being operated by the passenger

BOOK CARRIER In a suitable location, say the side of the elevator shaft, may be another shaft extending down to the basement, along which may run a closed box containing an endless chain or other suitable automatic book carrier, serving all of the stack decks and the terminal or delivery station. The carrier may be driven by power taken from the local steam, electric, or hydraulic plant, and running continually and quietly, transport with dispatch, books or other light matter both ways between the reading room and the stack without dependence on foot messengers. Such an apparatus, combined with the telephone, pneumatic tube, or other signal of any desired kind, does away with much of the fatigue and waste of time formerly unavoidable in the service of readers

HEATING AND VENTILATION The stack is warmed and ventilated by radiators, preferably of warm water, and auxiliary fans located underneath in the basement. Sufficient fresh out-door air is admitted into this chamber through filters, whence it passes through the basement floor and circulates upward and downward in the stacks through the deck slits. Discharge outlets are provided at the roof, controlled by hand and by thermostats

BOOK STACK AND SHELVING FOR LIBRARIES

AIR CLEANING OR DUSTING   If stacks are kept closed with automatic swing doors, no dust will come in from outside, and only that produced by use of the stack and handling the books will have to be dealt with. Occasional removal of dust is possible by compressed or exhaust air methods.

GENERAL CONSIDERATIONS   The peculiar compactness and simplicity of the construction and arrangement of this book stack renders it entirely feasible to carry it up an indefinite number of stories and thus utilize space and light generally unattainable on or near the ground   With proper foundation and supports the stack may be put on top of the building where light is plentiful, leaving the lower stories available for other purposes, even many of those of the library itself   The new stacks of the Congressional Library, which are nine stories or tiers in height, might as well have been nineteen if required   The quick and handy modern elevator, the automatic book carrier, the electric telephone, and pneumatic tube, etc , render the lofty book stack, as well as the lofty modern office building, equally useful and convenient in every part

It is hardly necessary to mention that the low shelving of but one or two tiers in height, which is sufficient for the needs of small libraries, such as those of city districts, towns, smaller colleges, etc , is readily constructed on the same plan as the lofty stack

HOW ALL THE REQUISITES OF THE PERFECT BOOK STACK AND SHELVING ARE EMBODIED IN THIS DESIGN   1   The uniformity in size of shelves, the ready doubling of their width at will, and their close adjustment to any desired height admit the shelving of books of any size or mixture of sizes whatever either standing on edge or lying flat, equally accessible and easily handled   If any shelf prove too wide, so that the books are liable to be pushed back out of sight, a wire or cord stretched behind and attached to the openwork partitions will hold them in place

2   The shelves are all precisely alike, made from one and the same pattern, and may be removed or dropped into place almost as quickly as a book can be   Any one or any number of the shelves may be removed, even while full of books, if the books be not too heavy, readjusted or interchanged, at any moment without the slightest interference with any other shelf or its contents

THE SNEAD AND COMPANY IRON WORKS

This is rendered feasible, expeditious and convenient by the absence of anything to be adjusted to receive the shelf or any catches, pins, or other movable supports for which one must search or feel. All annoyance of dropping movable pieces on the floor or down among the books is entirely avoided.

No shelf can slip off or tilt on its bearings. It may even be shifted with one hand while the other is otherwise occupied. Moreover, no shelf can be dislodged by any force from below or lifted off its bearings more than about three-eighths of an inch, because it is then stopped by the next tooth above on the support.

System Adapted to Any Classification

3   The shelves, once arranged for any particular classification of books, may be quickly and easily rearranged and shifted for any other.

All Books Accessible

4   Every book can be reached or its title read, without climbing or stepping above the floor or deck.

5   The main corridors of the stack room, the stairways and lifts, afford access to the books and free communication throughout the several tiers, and additional passages can be secured through the ranges themselves by merely removing the shelves.

Book Support

6   The book support or brace as applied to these shelves is by far the best ever devised. It depends solely upon its own shelf for attachment, is entirely independent of the spaces between shelves or the sizes of books, and is quickly and universally adjustable on any part of the shelf. It may face either way, and a pair of them may be so placed as to isolate a few books in the middle of the shelf. It may also be attached to bottom of a shelf and hang downward, to secure the tops of the books on the shelf below. It is equally applicable and useful on wooden shelves.

Maximum Capacity Secured

7   It is evident from the illustrations that a maximum of capacity and of indefinite vertical extension of the stack are secured by the general system described. On account of the minimum of space occupied by the shelf supports a saving in book storage capacity of 5% or more is made compared with most other systems.

Cleaning Simple

8   The simplicity of form and surface of the shelves and shelf supports, the only parts of the construction with which the books come in contact, render them very simple to polish and keep clean.

Thoroughly Fireproof

9   The construction entirely and economically avoids the use of any combustible material whatever, and also every connection with anything to cause fire, through the warming or the artificial lighting apparatus or otherwise.

Open Construction Diffuses Light

10   It is evident from the accompanying illustrations of the Congressional Library stacks that the location and sizes of the windows, in connection with the

BOOK STACK AND SHELVING FOR LIBRARIES

spacing and arrangement of the ranges and shelving, are such as to admit ample daylight to all parts of the shelving, even when filled solidly with books. As it seldom occurs, however, that some unfilled spaces do not exist on or between the shelves, the open skeleton construction of this system of shelving adds materially to the penetration and diffusion of light. The same is greatly enhanced also by the deck slits through which a great deal of light comes obliquely down directly from the sky through every upper window in the same range on both sides to the top of the stack. White marble decks and ceilings still further increase the illumination by reflection, and the stacks are well lighted at night by incandescent ceiling lamps in the aisles.

11. Dust is excluded by sealed windows, and by filters for the air admitted for ventilation. That which may be brought in with the books or otherwise, or which is produced by handling the books, is of small amount. The permanently sealed windows are an absolute security against damage from thunder showers, and from winds or gusts laden with dust or moisture.

12. The open grating of the shelves prevents the deposit of dust upon them, and therefore its accumulation at the back of the shelf, whence it is pushed by the books, as occurs with solid shelves. Roaches and other pests find on such a shelf but poor lodgment and much more light and air than they enjoy, while the books themselves, especially those much used, are benefited by the superior ventilation afforded.

13. The top tier of each shelf range is capped with a flanged sheet steel plate, which will shed any water that may leak through the roof or floor above, and thus secure the books at all times from such a source of injury.

14. By means of the deck slits, so evenly and liberally distributed throughout the stack, the open spaces through the decks at the window recesses, the extensive surface of window glass, and proper adjustable openings in the ceiling and lower floor, an ample circulation of air and nearly uniform temperature are secured throughout the stack. In very lofty stacks, a fan here and there may be needed in some situations, in summer weather.

15. By removing the shelves from any range section a free and direct passage is made through from range to range, which may be extended the entire length of the stack.

The deck slits or slots in front of the ranges, being about five inches wide, are

THE SNEAD AND COMPANY IRON WORKS

most convenient for attendants to talk through to each other, even through several stories, and to pass books or other small articles through from deck to deck either above or below

Books may be shelved as low down as the floor or deck level without danger of injury to the bindings from sweeping or washing of the deck or of abrasion from passing trucks, because effectually guarded by the raised curb and intervening slot in the deck

This convenience is wanting in the continuous deck, and the slits are unobjectionable Articles are very rarely, if ever, dropped through, and then will never fall more than one story, while it is impossible for a person to step through without special effort It has also been proved by experience that the deck slit does not expose attendants on one of the upper decks to the view of those below

16 The open arrangement of the framework permits the use of any range section or any number of them at any time for catalogue cabinets, closets, cases of drawers, small desks or tables, etc The simple removal of the shelves renders these spaces thus available at a moment's notice.

Every window in the range passages may contain a spacious permanent seat, in the full light, suited for the accommodation of the attendants or of special students who may be admitted to the stack

A ledge of six inches or more in width may readily be hung on the front of any book range, as a rest, and be quickly removed at will The front teeth of the shelf supports furnish convenient and adjustable attachments for this purpose (fig 5, page 27)

Movable tables running on casters may also be used in the corridors

17 It is believed to be impossible to devise a construction simpler in every sense of the word, or more economically manufactured and installed, than that here described, fulfilling the essential requisites of either a large book stack or a small system of shelving in one tier

The cost in any case cannot exceed that of any other design for a good quality of workmanship and materials At the same time the design lends itself to any degree of ornamental and elegant treatment that may be desirable for conspicuous or special locations

18 The automatic book carrier, elevator, pneumatic tube, and telephone furnish quick and direct communication between the stack and the reading or cataloguing rooms

BOOK STACK AND SHELVING FOR LIBRARIES

SHELVING FOR SMALL LIBRARIES AND BOOK CASES Reference to figures 24, 25, 26 and 29 will show how the shelves and supports, used for the large library or book stack, are entirely suited to any desired arrangement of shelving on a smaller scale, without loss of any of the advantages possessed by stack shelving

The framework may be bolted together so as to be knocked down for removal, and the several parts, being chiefly bars and flat castings, of but few shapes and sizes, snugly packed into the smallest compass

Book shelving must always be pretty much the same thing whether in the form of a small book case, a small one-story library, or a book stack of any extent Most of the parts, therefore, will be of standard shapes and sizes

GENERALLY The adaptability of a properly designed book stack is as universal as the possibility of storing any large quantity of books in a classified and accessible arrangement This is apparent on examination of the Green system of shelving It can be placed anywhere, in single or double-faced arrangement, is readily carried by floors or foundations of any sort, because its weight is uniformly distributed over the area and there are no important concentrated load points This incidentally renders the stack a most economical support itself of stories and roof above, if desired

The main reading room floor of the new great Public Library of New York rests directly on the book stack, seven tiers in height, just beneath it

This stack structure is also so inconspicuous of itself, due to its light, skeleton form, that, when filled with books, practically nothing is visible but solid tiers of books with decks between them, forming a real stack of books

It is, moreover, a self-sustaining structure and needs essentially but a foundation or floor to stand on, or even to be suspended from, if that were desirable in any case The walls and roof, as for an ice house, are needed only for protection from the weather and practically not at all for support

Such a structure is a true book stack

It is built within a building and is not necessarily any part of it, — merely its furniture or content

Its minimum internal dimensions and relations of parts are determined by the sizes of the books and the stature of the persons who use it A newspaper or map

THE SNEAD AND COMPANY IRON WORKS

stack would be different internally from a stack for the ordinary sizes of books because the material to be shelved is more bulky

With electric illumination under convenient control, daylight is no longer indispensable and the stack may be located anywhere and be of any dimensions, regardless of daylight or exposure to fire

The location is thus no longer a serious architectural or administrative question, and the Green stack easily lends itself to the solution of every problem of this nature

The undersigned are fully prepared to manufacture the book stacks, shelving, and book supports above described, and to submit designs and estimates for adapting them to any situation where fireproof, or even semi-fireproof construction (iron framework and supports with wooden shelves) is required

Correspondence is solicited from architects, trustees of libraries, or librarians, contemplating the erection of new libraries, or the modification or enlargement of existing shelving or book stacks

THE SNEAD & CO IRON WORKS
(Incorporated)
JERSEY CITY, N J

BOOK STACK AND SHELVING FOR LIBRARIES

PARTIAL LIST OF LIBRARIES USING THE GREEN SYSTEM OF BOOK STACK AND SHELVING

LIBRARY OF CONGRESS
WASHINGTON, D C
SMITHMEYER & PELZ and EDWARD P CASEY, Architects

NEW YORK PUBLIC LIBRARY
NEW YORK CITY
CARRERE & HASTINGS, Architects

CONVERSE MEMORIAL LIBRARY
MALDEN, MASS
SHEPLEY, RUTAN & COOLIDGE, Architects

CARNEGIE PUBLIC LIBRARY
WASHINGTON, D C
ALBERT RANDOLPH ROSS, Architect

LELAND STANFORD JR UNIVERSITY LIBRARY
STANFORD UNIVERSITY, CAL
CHARLES EDWARD HODGES, Architect

CARNEGIE PUBLIC LIBRARY
SYRACUSE, N Y
JAMES A RANDALL Architect

PUBLIC REFERENCE LIBRARY
TORONTO, ONTARIO
WICKSON & GREGG and A H CHAPMAN, Architects

KRAUTH MEMORIAL LIBRARY
LUTHERAN THEOLOGICAL SEMINARY, MT AIRY, PHILADELPHIA, PA
WATSON & HUCKEL, Architects

LOUISVILLE FREE PUBLIC LIBRARY
LOUISVILLE, KY
PILCHER & TACHAU, Architects

PORTLAND PUBLIC LIBRARY
PORTLAND, ME
F H FASSETT, Architect

Y M C A LIBRARY
NEW YORK CITY
PARISH & SCHROEDER, Architects

PARLIAMENTARY LIBRARY
WELLINGTON, N Z
JOHN CAMPBELL, Gov Architect

THE SNEAD AND COMPANY IRON WORKS

MASONIC LIBRARY
BOSTON, MASS
LORING & PHIPPS, Architects

AMERICAN SOCIETY OF CIVIL ENGINEERS
NEW YORK CITY
C J W EIDLITZ Architect

KANSAS STATE AGRICULTURAL COLLEGE
MANHATTAN, KAN
SEYMOUR DAVIS, Architect

NEW HAMPSHIRE STATE LIBRARY
CONCORD, N H
A P CUTTING, Architect

BLACKSTONE MEMORIAL LIBRARY
BRANFORD, CONN
S S BEMAN, Architect

INDIANA STATE NORMAL SCHOOL
TERRA HAUTE, IND
W L B JENNEY and W H LOYD, Architects

LIBRARY OF THE NEW YORK LAW ASSOCIATION, U S P O BLDG
NEW YORK CITY
U S Supervising Architect

FALL RIVER PUBLIC LIBRARY
FALL RIVER, MASS
CRAM, GOODHUE & FERGUSON, Architects

VIRGINIA STATE LIBRARY
RICHMOND, VA
W M POINDEXTER, Architect

PUBLIC LIBRARY
CANTON, MASS
WINSLOW & BIGELOW, Architects

RIDGEFIELD MEMORIAL LIBRARY
RIDGEFIELD, CONN
RALEIGH C GILDERSLEEVE, Architect

GENERAL THEOLOGICAL SEMINARY
NEW YORK CITY
CHAS C HAIGHT, Architect

FLOWER MEMORIAL LIBRARY
WATERTOWN, N Y
ORCHARD, LANSING & JORALEMON, Architects
J & R LAMB, Interior Decorators

[18]

BOOK STACK AND SHELVING FOR LIBRARIES

JEWISH THEOLOGICAL SEMINARY
NEW YORK CITY
ARNOLD W BRUNNER, Architect

ROCHESTER THEOLOGICAL SEMINARY
ROCHESTER, N Y
J FOSTER WARNER, Architect

EVANSTON PUBLIC LIBRARY
EVANSTON, ILL
JAS GAMBLE ROGERS and CHAS A PHILLIPS, Architects

AMERICAN SOCIETY FOR PREVENTION OF CRUELTY TO ANIMALS
NEW YORK CITY
RENWICK, ASPINWALL & OWEN, Architects

HYDE PARK LIBRARY
HYDE PARK, MASS
CLARKE & RUSSELL Architects

MAINE HISTORICAL SOCIETY
PORTLAND, ME
F H FASSETT Architect

APPELLATE COURT LIBRARY
MT VERNON, ILL

SCHOOL OF MINES & METALLURGY
ROLLA, MO
HOWE, HOIT, and CUTLER, Architects

UNIVERSITY OF PENNSYLVANIA LIBRARY
PHILADELPHIA, PA
FURNESS & EVANS, Architects

PUBLIC LIBRARY
WHEELING, W VA

FLETCHER LIBRARY
WESTFORD, MASS
H M FRANCIS, Architect

PUBLIC LIBRARY
EXETER, N H
ROTCH & TILDEN, Architects

THE WESTERN COLLEGE FOR WOMEN
OXFORD, OHIO
RENWICK, ASPINWALL & RUSSELL Architects

PUBLIC LIBRARY
LITTLETON, MASS
PERKINS & BETTON, Architects

THE SNEAD AND COMPANY IRON WORKS

PACIFIC BRANCH LIBRARY
BROOKLYN, N Y
RAYMOND F ALMIRALL, Architect

CARROLL PARK BRANCH LIBRARY
BROOKLYN, N Y
WM B TUBBS & BRO, Architects

WILLIAMSBURG BRANCH LIBRARY
BROOKLYN, N Y
WALKER & MORRIS, Architects

ARMY WAR COLLEGE
WASHINGTON, D C
McKIM, MEAD & WHITE, Architects

AMERICAN PHILOSOPHICAL SOCIETY
PHILADELPHIA, PA
FRANK MILES DAY & BRO, Architects

PUBLIC LIBRARY
SYDNEY, NEW SOUTH WALES

N Y GENEALOGICAL & BIOGRAPHICAL SOCIETY
NEW YORK CITY

U S NAVAL HOME
PHILADELPHIA, PA

BENEDICT COLLEGE LIBRARY
COLUMBIA, S C

DEPARTMENT OF AGRICULTURE
WASHINGTON, D C
RANKIN, KELLOGG & CRANE, Architects

UNION THEOLOGICAL SEMINARY
NEW YORK CITY
ALLEN & COLLENS, Architects

ACADEMY OF NATURAL SCIENCES
PHILADELPHIA, PA
WILSON, HARRIS & RICHARDS, Architects

COLLEGE OF PHYSICIANS
PHILADELPHIA, PA
COPE & STEWARDSON, Architects

THE SNEAD AND COMPANY IRON WORKS

LIBRARY OF CONGRESS, WASHINGTON, D. C.
(Figures 1, 2 and 3)

THESE general drawings of the North Stack, Library of Congress, are referred to in the preceding pages and illustrate a typical arrangement of the bookstack for a large library. Additional stairways and book lifts can be introduced if found desirable.

A number of typical library plans will be found in the pages following.

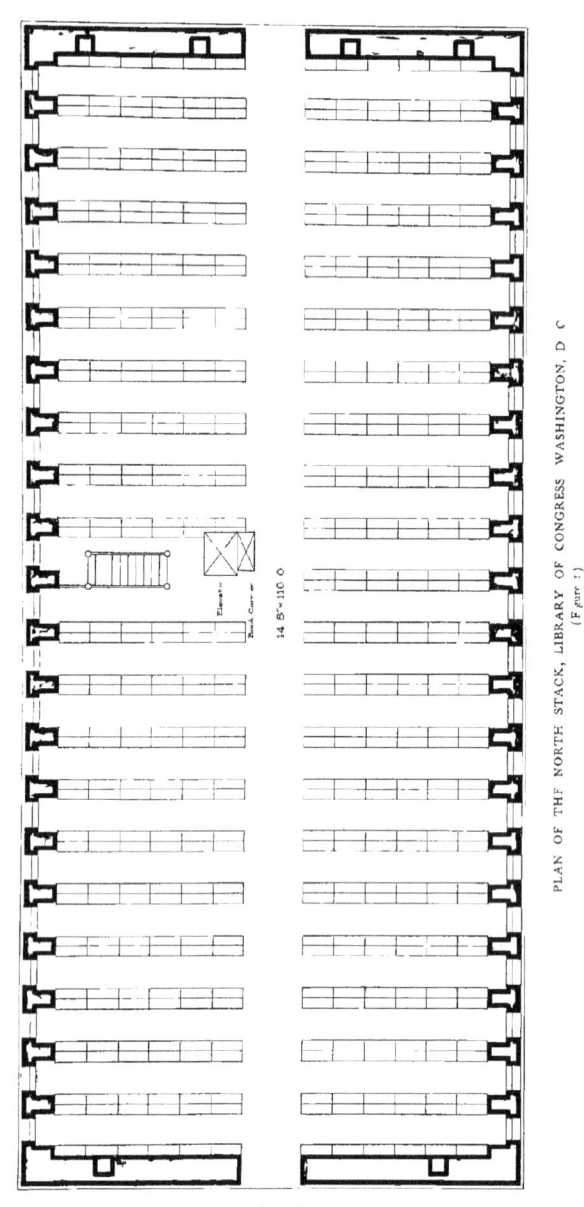

BOOK STACK AND SHELVING FOR LIBRARIES

PLAN OF THE NORTH STACK, LIBRARY OF CONGRESS WASHINGTON, D C
(Fig. 1)

THE SNEAD AND COMPANY IRON WORKS

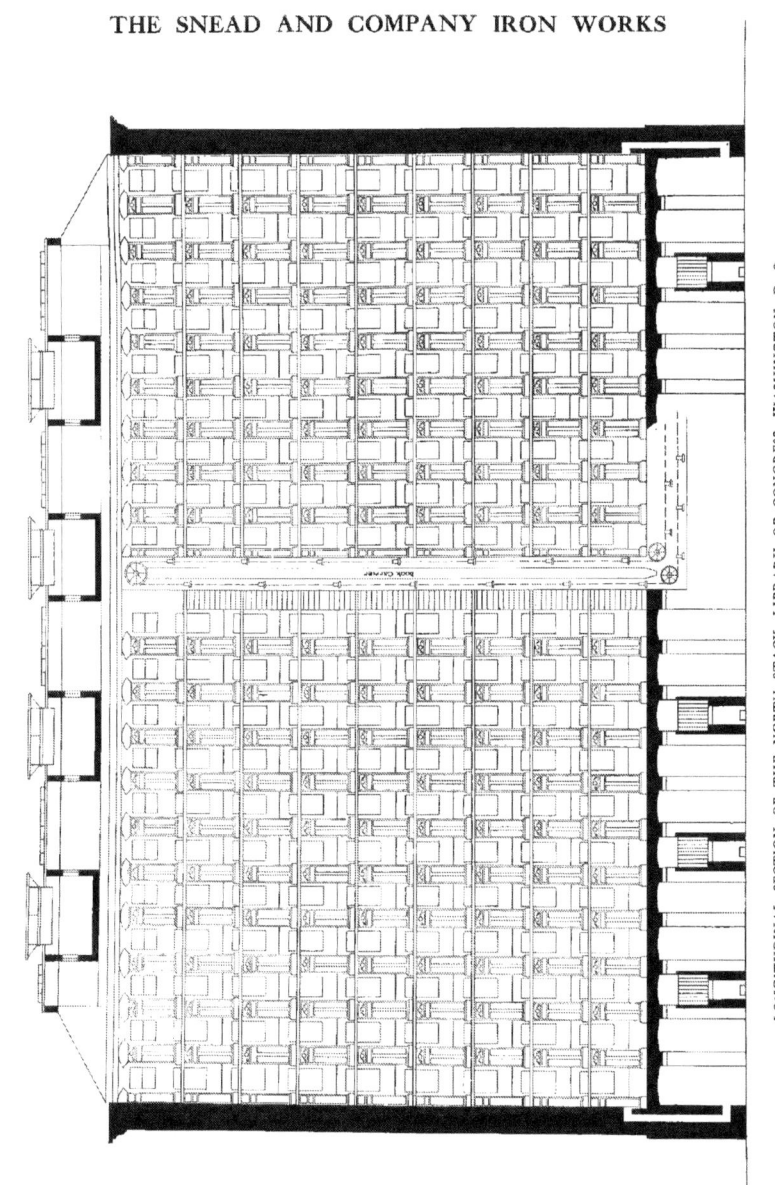

LONGITUDINAL SECTION OF THE NORTH STACK, LIBRARY OF CONGRESS, WASHINGTON, D. C.
(Figure 2)

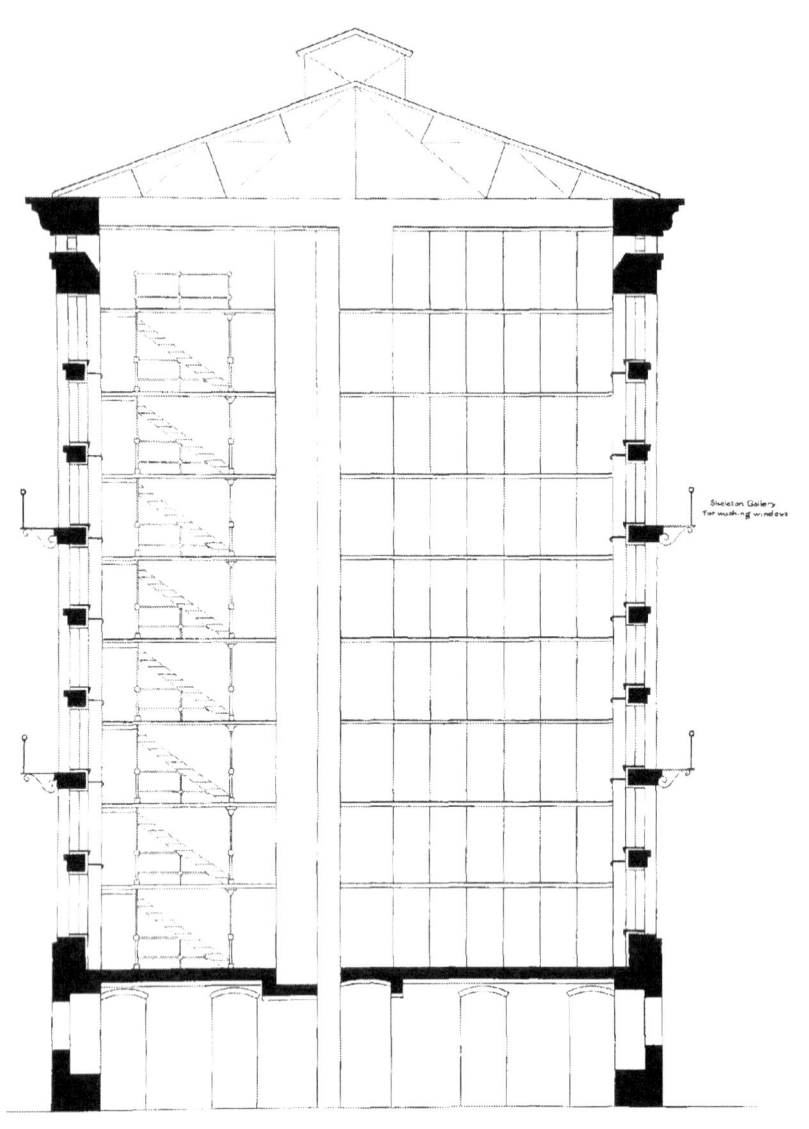

BOOK STACK AND SHELVING FOR LIBRARIES

CROSS SECTION OF THE NORTH STACK, LIBRARY OF CONGRESS, WASHINGTON, D. C.
(Figure 3)

THE SNEAD AND COMPANY IRON WORKS

RANGE FRONT AND INTERMEDIATE SHELF SUPPORT
(Figures 4 and 5)

THESE illustrate the typical supports for 10-inch shelves, the end support being called a range front. Each support is of a single thickness of cast iron, perforated as shown, and the range front may be ornamented to suit the taste of the architect, see also figures 9, 17 and 19. Cast iron is the most important and the most necessary of all productions in metal. Its uses are multifarious, from the heavy structural parts in buildings, engines and machines to the beautiful and delicate architectural forms that adorn the interior and exterior of our finest edifices.

The standard tier height is 7 ft 0 in from floor to floor, this being the limit for easy reaching of books and reading of titles on the upper shelves. The tier can be made 7 ft 6 in high if desired.

In figure 5 the horns for supporting the back of the shelf are shown cast on the shelf support; these can as well be of steel and placed on the vertical stiffening rib of the support, see also figures 13 and 15.

For half-tone illustration of a range with shelf supports shown in figures 4 and 5, see figure 25.

BOOK STACK AND SHELVING FOR LIBRARIES

Deck Floor Line

Deck Slit

7'0" Standard Height can be made 7'6"

Portable Ledge

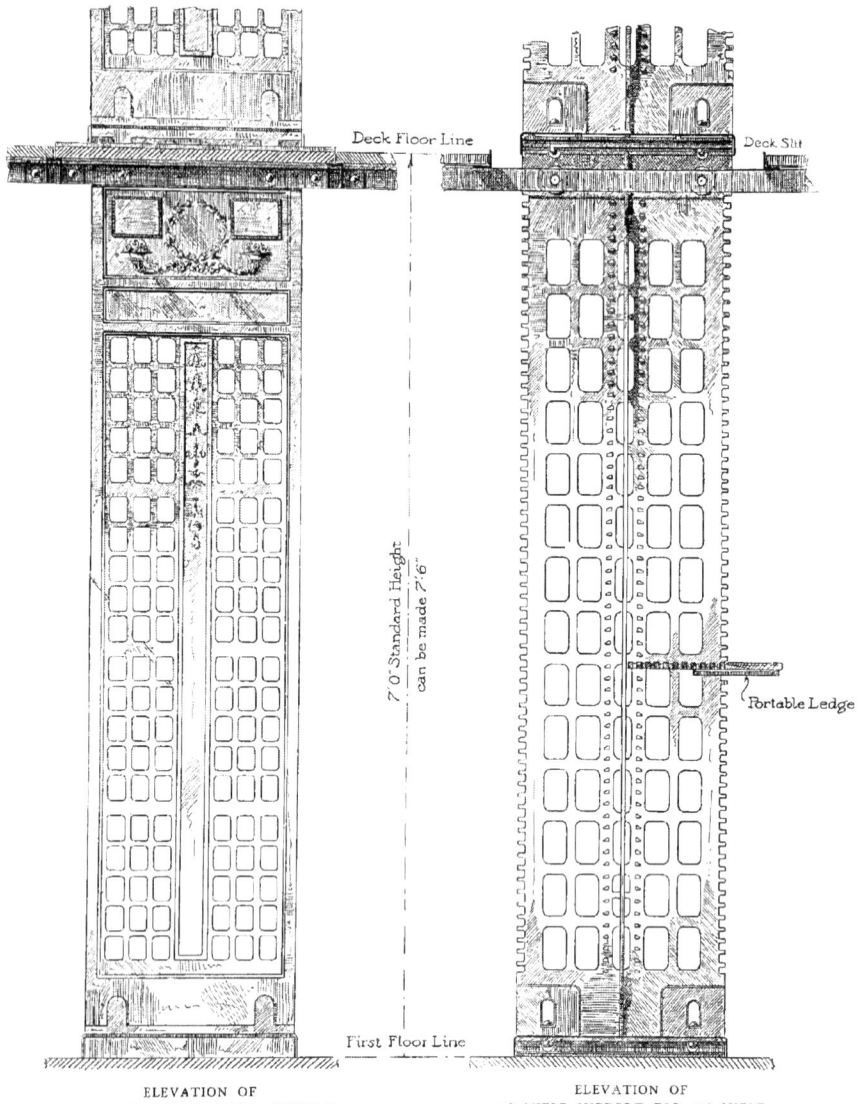

First Floor Line

ELEVATION OF
10" RANGE FRONT FOR 10" SHELF
(Figure 4)

ELEVATION OF
10" SHELF SUPPORT FOR 10" SHELF
(Figure 5)

THE SNEAD AND COMPANY IRON WORKS

SKELETON SHELF, BOOK SUPPORT AND PORTABLE LEDGE

(Figures 6 and 7)

THE mechanical construction of the shelf and book support are shown generally For complete description of the shelf see page 48, and for half-tone illustrations see figures 21 and 22.

In figure 6 a steel column is shown in connection with the shelf support, this construction may be employed when the stack is unusually high or carries heavy loads above it.

BOOK STACK AND SHELVING FOR LIBRARIES

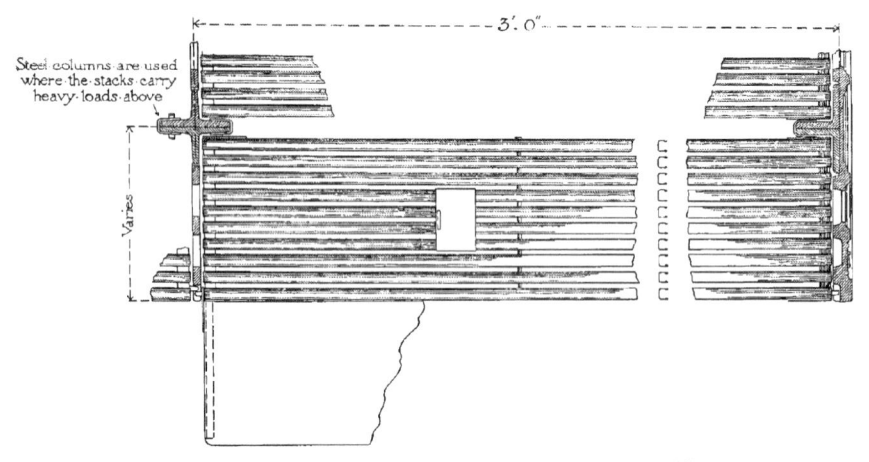

Steel columns are used where the stacks carry heavy loads above

PLAN OF BOOK SHELF, BOOK SUPPORT AND PORTABLE LEDGE
(Figure 6)

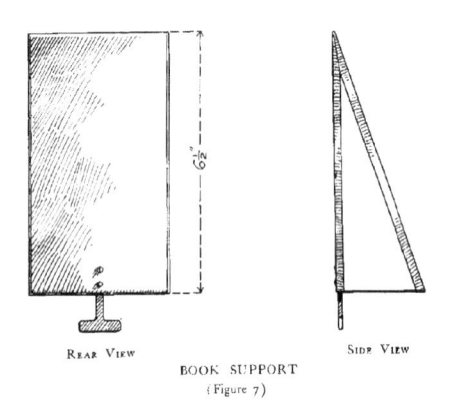

Rear View Side View

BOOK SUPPORT
(Figure 7)

THE SNEAD AND COMPANY IRON WORKS

PLAN OF DECK AND RANGES
(Figure 8)

THE relative positions of shelf supports, shelves, corridor, aisle, deck slits and window seat are shown in this enlarged plan.

The shelf supports are but 7/16 of an inch thick and thereby consume a minimum amount of space, resulting in a maximum book storage capacity for our stack, being the full depth of the shelf compartment the supports brace the end books and the shelves are carried at their extreme outer corners.

The shelves are not more than 3/4 of an inch apart at their back edges, this prevents small books from falling between and makes a through shelf for large books where opposite shelves are placed at the same level.

Deck slits are usually 4 or 5 inches wide, they afford circulation of air and communication between decks, effect a saving in the cost of marble or glass flooring, and their curb angles prevent damage to books on the lower shelves from the feet, book trucks or the mopping of deck floor.

See also figures 19 and 20.

BOOK STACK AND SHELVING FOR LIBRARIES

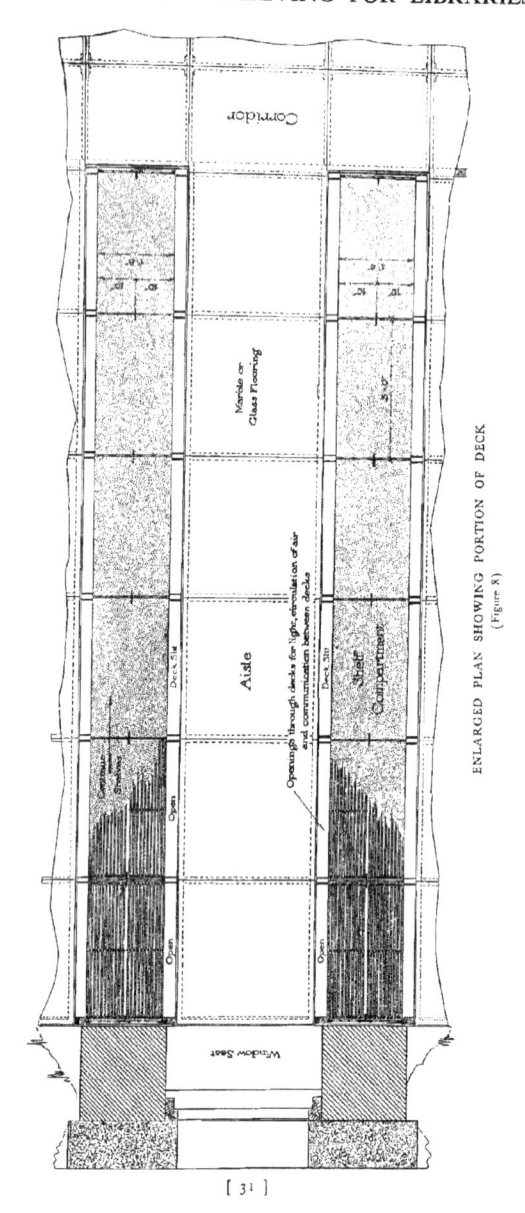

ENLARGED PLAN SHOWING PORTION OF DECK
(Figure 8)

THE SNEAD AND COMPANY IRON WORKS

RANGE FRONTS
(Figures 9 and 10)

THE designs shown here can be furnished if preferred to figure 4, or architects can make their own design The narrow panel near the top can be made movable so as to be used as a card frame

Where it is desired to have separate control for the electric lights in each aisle between the ranges the vertical conduits and switch box may be carried up concealed in the sheet steel duct shown in figure 10, these ducts are removable A more economical method of controlling the aisle lights is by means of hanging tassel switches which do not require the iron ducts

For half-tone illustration of a range with front as shown in figure 9, see figure 24

BOOK STACK AND SHELVING FOR LIBRARIES

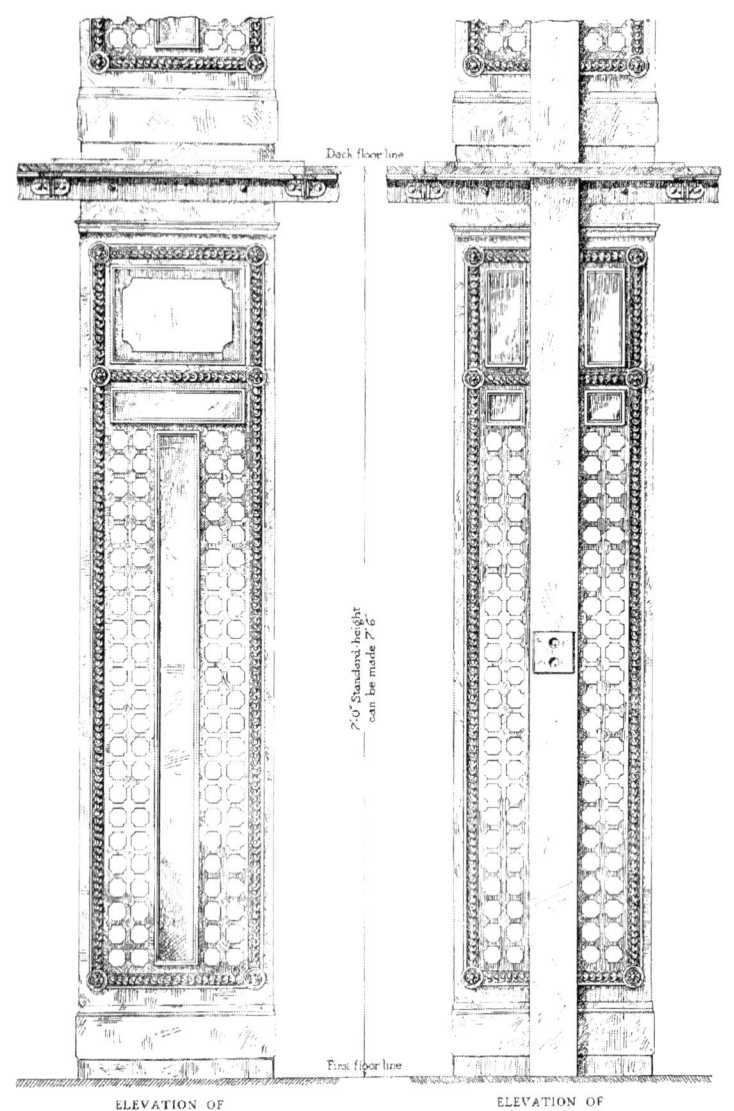

ELEVATION OF
20″ RANGE FRONT FOR 10″ SHELF
(Figure 9)

ELEVATION OF
20″ RANGE FRONT FOR 10″ SHELF
SHOWING DUCT FOR ELECTRIC WIRES
(Figure 10)

THE SNEAD AND COMPANY IRON WORKS

RANGE FRONTS
(Figures 11 and 12)

THIS design is similar to figures 9 and 10, but is shown adapted to an 8-inch shelf and only one tier high with cornice. For stacks of two or more tiers the upper tier is finished as here shown.

BOOK STACK AND SHELVING FOR LIBRARIES

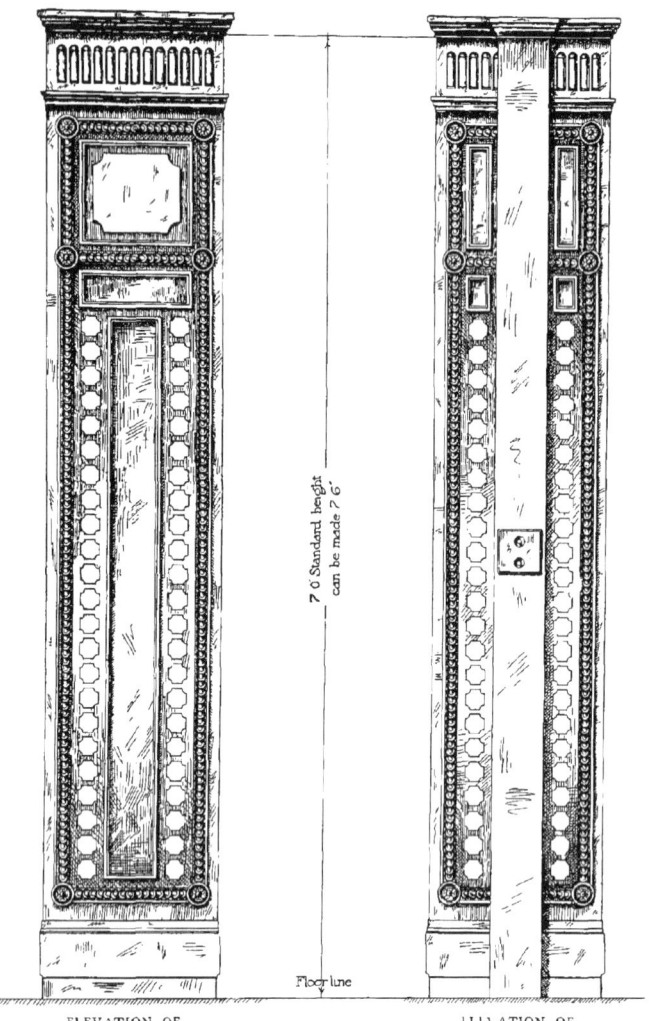

7'0" Standard height can be made 7'6"

Floor line

ELEVATION OF
16" RANGE FRONT FOR 8" SHELF
(Figure 11)

ELEVATION OF
16" RANGE FRONT FOR 8" SHELF
SHOWING DUCT FOR ELECTRIC WIRES
(Figure 12)

THE SNEAD AND COMPANY IRON WORKS

INTERMEDIATE SHELF SUPPORTS
(Figures 13 and 14)

THE 20-inch shelf support, figure 13, is similar to that shown in figure 5 except that the shelf-supporting horns are made of steel and placed on the stiffening rib of the shelf support. See figure 15.

The shelf support for eight-inch shelves is here shown with the cast iron horns (see also figure 16), but the steel construction can be used as well.

For half-tone illustrations of intermediate shelf supports in a range see figures 24 and 25.

BOOK STACK AND SHELVING FOR LIBRARIES

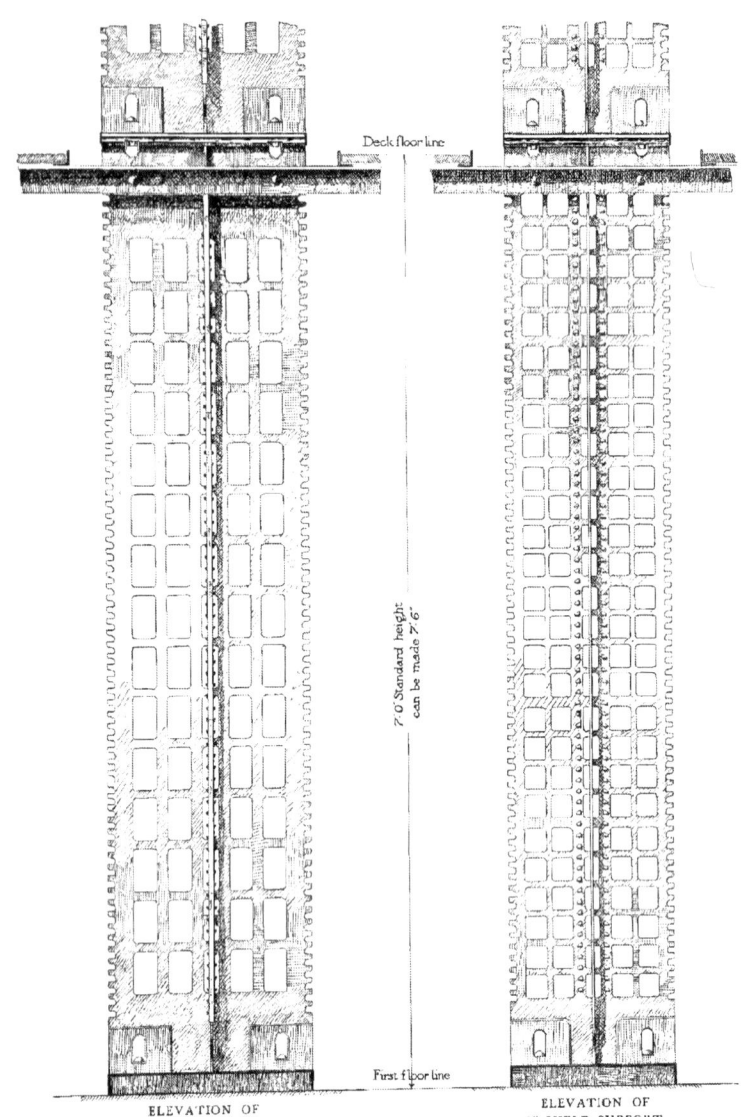

ELEVATION OF
20″ SHELF SUPPORT
SHOWING SMALL STEEL SUPPORTING HORNS AT BACK OF SHELF
(Figure 13)

ELEVATION OF
16″ SHELF SUPPORT
SHOWING SMALL CAST IRON SUPPORTING HORNS AT BACK OF SH
(Figure 14)

THE SNEAD AND COMPANY IRON WORKS

DETAIL SHOWING CONSTRUCTION AND SPECIAL FEATURES

(Key to figures 15 and 16)

(A) Open work shelf support, permitting free circulation of air and moderate light throughout the stack. It is only 7/16-inch thick, giving a maximum space for books, of solid construction with no enclosed spaces for storing dust or harboring vermin

(B) Skeleton cold rolled steel adjustable shelf, also permitting free circulation of air throughout the stack, of minimum weight and maximum strength for supporting its load without deflection

These shelves always lie level, they never get in wind or rattle on their bearings

(C) Tooth for supporting fronts of shelves—the shelves of adjoining compartments can rest on the same tooth, permitting a thin support and doing away with lost space

(D) Interlocking device or horn, securing the shelf in its place and preventing its dislodgment when in position

(E) Book support, a rigid adjustable brace for books on partially filled shelves

(F) Diaphragm forming bottom shelf and a continuous brace at deck floors throughout the stack, also a fire, dust and water stop

(G) Deck slit generally 4 to 5 inches wide for circulation of air from deck to deck and for communication between decks

(H) Curb angle for receiving floor of marble or glass and for preventing the injury of books on bottom shelves by floor mop, book truck or the feet of attendants

(I) Deck floor of marble or glass or any other suitable material

(J) Deck floor girder

BOOK STACK AND SHELVING FOR LIBRARIES

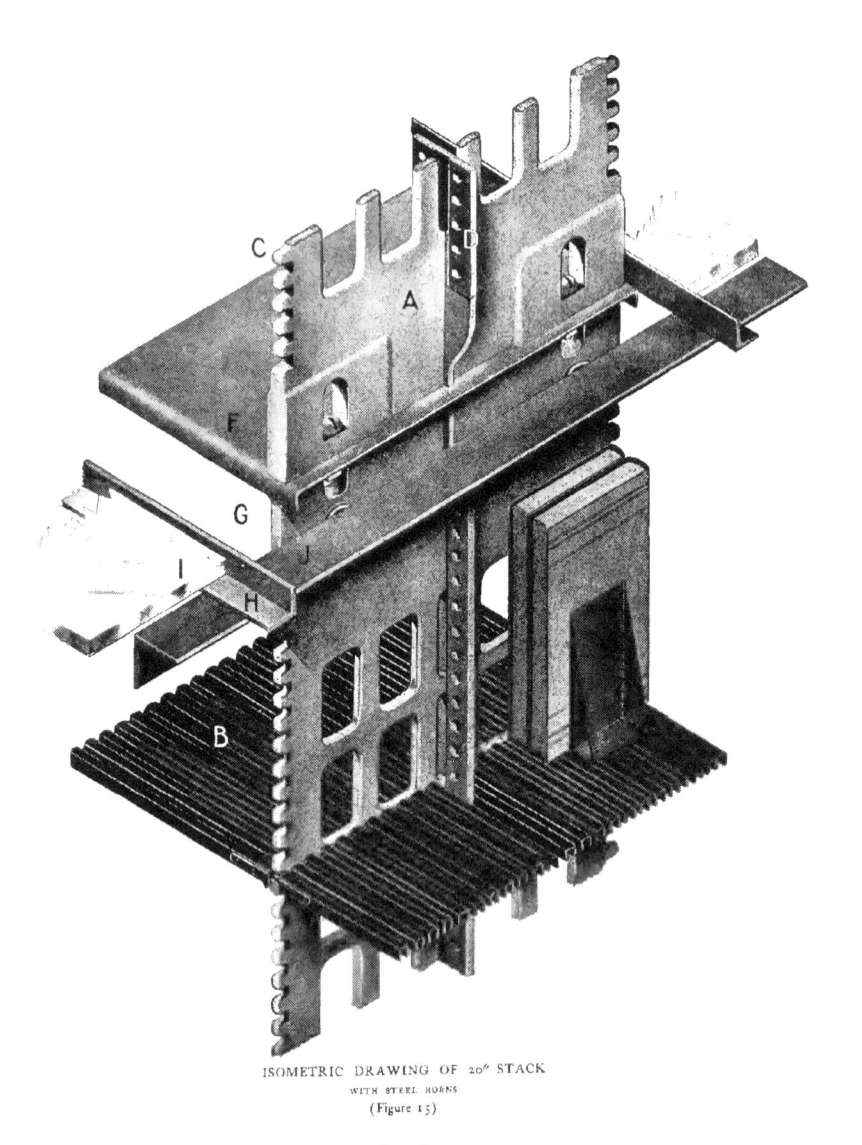

ISOMETRIC DRAWING OF 20″ STACK
WITH STEEL HORNS
(Figure 15)

THE SNEAD AND COMPANY IRON WORKS

DETAIL SHOWING CONSTRUCTION AND SPECIAL FEATURES
(Figure 16)

FOR key see preceding page. While the steel horns are shown for the twenty-inch stack and cast iron horns for the sixteen-inch stack, either construction can be adapted to each width of stack; each performs its functions, viz., supporting the shelf, interlocking it and preventing its dislodgment by a blow or pull. The horns are all rounded and are out of the way of books and there is no liability of injury to books from either one or the other.

BOOK STACK AND SHELVING FOR LIBRARIES

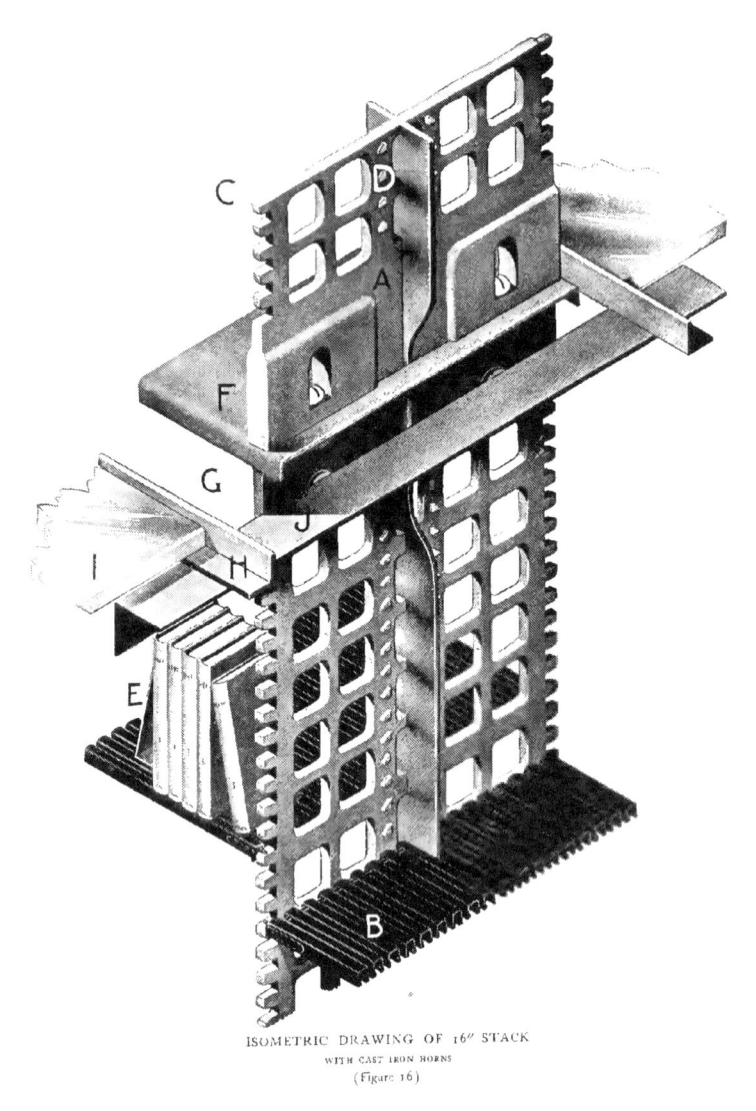

ISOMETRIC DRAWING OF 16″ STACK
WITH CAST IRON HORNS
(Figure 16)

THE SNEAD AND COMPANY IRON WORKS

NEW YORK PUBLIC LIBRARY
CARRERE & HASTINGS, Architects

RANGE FRONT, INTERMEDIATE SUPPORT AND DECK FLOOR

(Figures 17 and 18)

IN the design of range front shown in figure 17 provision is made for numerals and orientation letters in connection with the shelf classification, and immediately below these is a metal card frame open at the ends

Within the stack and forming a part of the shelf supports are steel columns (see figure 6), in the New York Public Library these columns extend up through seven tiers and carry the reading room floor immediately above the stack

BOOK STACK AND SHELVING FOR LIBRARIES

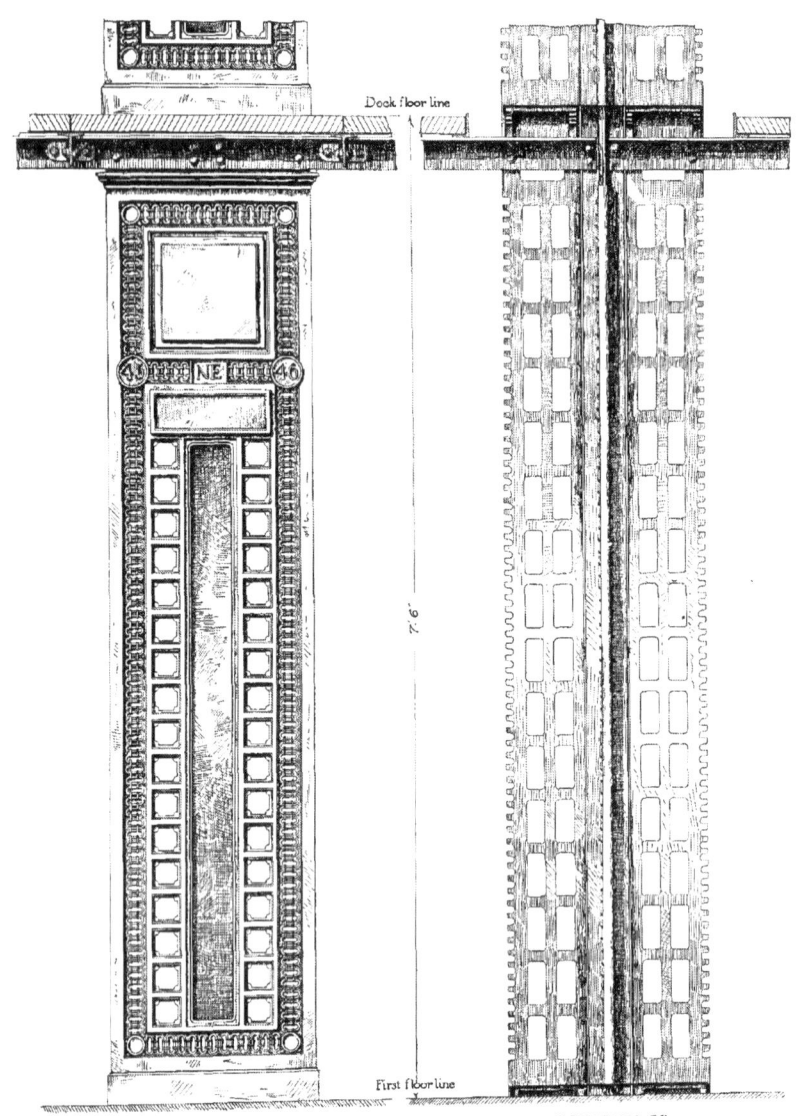

ELEVATION OF
19" RANGE FRONT FOR 9" SHELF
(Figure 17)

ELEVATION OF
19" SHELF SUPPORT FOR 9" SHELF
(Figure 18)

[43]

THE SNEAD AND COMPANY IRON WORKS

LIBRARY OF CONGRESS, WASHINGTON, D. C.
(Figure 19)

THIS shows practically the Library of Congress stack. Note the shelf ledge, window seat and deck slit. Refer to plan of deck, figure 8.

BOOK STACK AND SHELVING FOR LIBRARIES

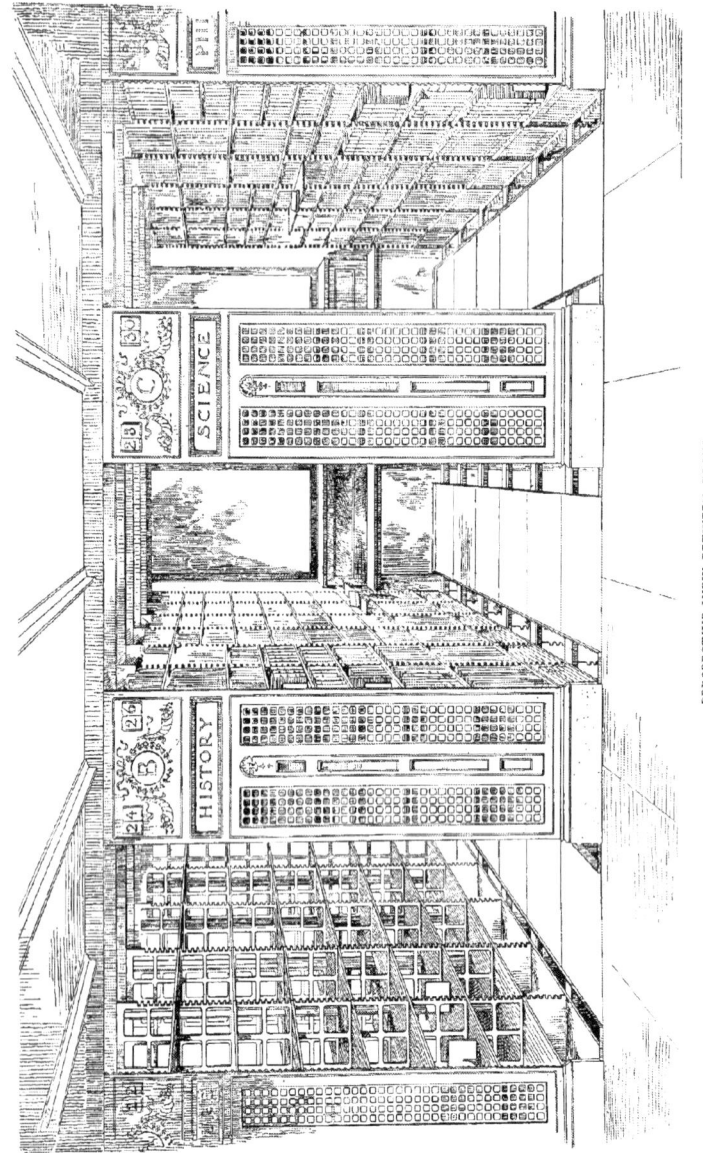

PERSPECTIVE VIEW BETWEEN DECKS
(Figure 19)

THE SNEAD AND COMPANY IRON WORKS

THE BOOK STACK
(Figure 20)

THE type of construction shown employs the steel column within the stack as described for figures 17 and 18. One great advantage of this construction is that it affords an opportunity of omitting the shelves and shelf supports in any tier or part of a tier, thereby resulting in economy of first cost, as the shelving can be added as required.

In either type of stack the shelves can be removed and the compartment utilized to form a passage through the stack or to receive a table resting on the bottom diaphragm plate.

IMPORTANT One of the officers in a large library was taken ill in January 1908 with smallpox. The building was promptly closed to the public and some parts, but especially the bookstack erected by The Snead and Co Iron Works, was disinfected with formaldehyde. The process was simple, owing to the open character of the stack, and there was not the slightest difficulty in the gas penetrating everywhere except between the leaves of closely packed and tightly closed books, this being due of course to the books themselves and not at all to the shelves which held them. The open slits of the decks and the open work of the structure comprising the range fronts, shelf supports, book supports and open bar shelves, and the entire absence of hollow enclosed spaces all made thorough disinfection possible.

BOOK STACK AND SHELVING FOR LIBRARIES

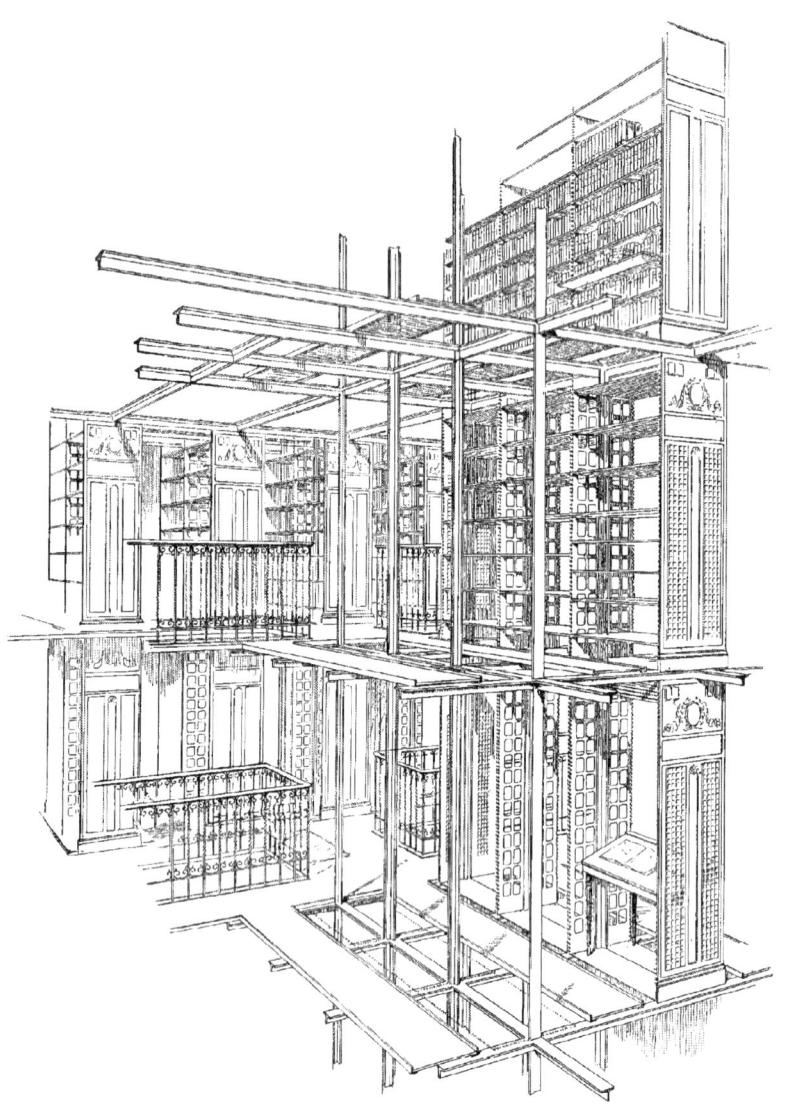

PERSPECTIVE VIEW OF STACK
(Figure 20)

THE SNEAD AND COMPANY IRON WORKS

SKELETON STEEL SHELF, BOOK SUPPORT AND LABEL HOLDER

(Figures 21 and 22)

ONE of the most important features of this system is the skeleton steel shelf which is illustrated on the opposite page. The construction is of very thin cold rolled steel, the bars being of inverted U section and the end pieces of L section, so connected as to be absolutely rigid when in place and capable of rough handling without loosening in any part. The shelf is made with a certain flexibility and resilience, preventing it from getting permanently in wind and becoming jammed between the supports, it always lies flat and cannot rattle on its bearings.

All surfaces, especially the top which receives the books, are as smooth as polished glass and the tops of the bars are broad and rounded, so that books slide or rest on them without the least injury. Every part is free from sharp edges or points. After the shelf is made it is covered with a baked enamel that protects it from rust or corrosion in contact with the books.

All shelves should be of the standard length of 3 feet and are 8 or 10 inches wide, they are thus adjustable and interchangeable throughout the stack. A standard 10-inch by 3-foot shelf weighs but 5½ pounds and will support a uniformly distributed load of 40 pounds per square foot without deflecting more than one-eighth of an inch. It is of uniform strength from front to back and does not derive its strength from a flange at the back and front, such as a sheet metal shelf.

The bar spaces furnish admirable attachment for the book supports and label holders and prevent accumulation of dust on the shelf; they add materially to the diffusion and penetration of light and to proper ventilation through the individual ranges.

Each shelf is complete in itself and there are no catches, pins or other movable supports for which one has to search or feel, and no screw driver or spirit level to be carried about in moving or adjusting the shelf.

TEST OF SKELETON STEEL SHELF, $10'' \times 3'$—$0''$

Center Load	Deflection
62 lbs	$\frac{1}{16}''$
105 "	$\frac{1}{8}''$
150 "	$\frac{3}{16}''$
207 "	$\frac{5}{16}''$
264 "	$\frac{3}{8}''$
325 "	$\frac{7}{16}''$
506 "	$\frac{1}{2}''$

When this load was removed the shelf resumed its original shape. The same shelf finally collapsed under a center load of 712 lbs.

Forty pounds per superficial foot equals 100 lbs. distributed load or 50 lbs. center load for this shelf.

BOOK STACK AND SHELVING FOR LIBRARIES

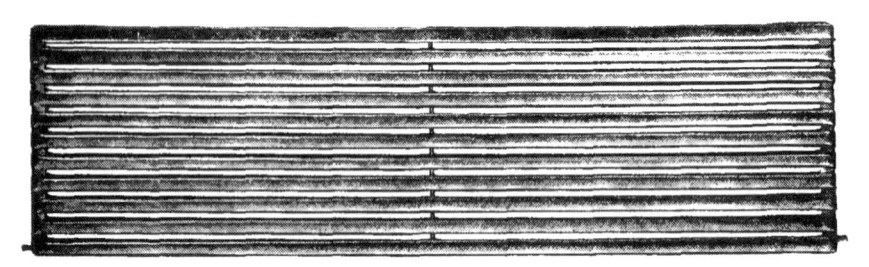

PLAN
(Figure 21)

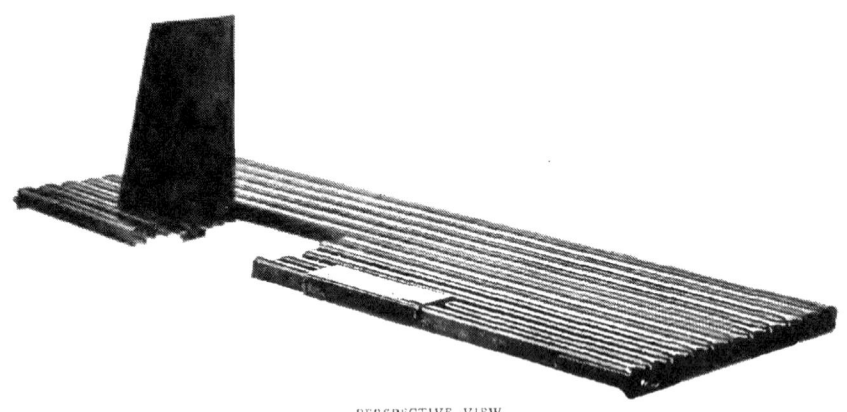

PERSPECTIVE VIEW
WITH SHELF CUT OUT TO SHOW ATTACHMENT OF BOOK SUPPORT AND LABEL HOLDER
(Figure 22)

THE SKELETON STEEL SHELF

THE SNEAD AND COMPANY IRON WORKS

ROLLER SHELF
(Figure 23)

FOR large volumes laid flat and where sliding shelves are not desired this roller shelf is the best and strongest made, the methods of supporting and adjusting it are the same as for the standard skeleton shelf

The shelf frame consists of steel angles and bars securely riveted together, the rollers are provided with fixed steel pins at ends that turn freely on their bearings

BOOK STACK AND SHELVING FOR LIBRARIES

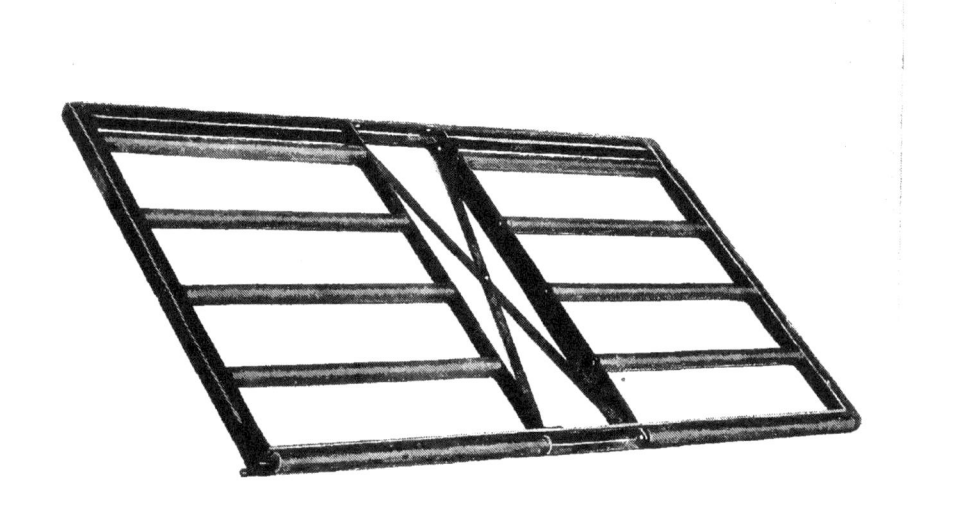

ROLLER SHELF
(Figure 23)

THE SNEAD AND COMPANY IRON WORKS
DOUBLE FACED RANGE OF TWO COMPARTMENTS
(Figure 24)

THIS illustrates a standard double faced range for 10-inch by 3-foot shelves with two compartments, the range being about 7½ feet high

The cast iron shelf supports are perforated, consistent with strength, to permit of the free circulation of light and air throughout the stack; they are about 7/16 of an inch in thickness, which considered in comparison with sheet metal construction gives a greater book storage capacity, generally about 4 per cent more

The range front can be ornamented as desired and, being perforated, lends itself to the ready adjustment on the outside, by hooks or brackets, of label holders, shelf lists, notices, drop desks, etc, all of which are conveniences in library work The narrow panel at the top can be provided with a metal card frame

All parts of the shelf supports are rounded and there are no sharp edges to injure bindings The whole construction is open There are no hollow enclosed inaccessible places where dust can accumulate and where rust can form or roaches and vermin be harbored

At the bottom of each compartment is a strong sheet steel diaphragm forming a shelf, where a stack is several tiers high this diaphragm serves as a continuation of the flooring to walk through the range whenever an open passage through any bay may be desired and is obtained by simply removing the shelves (see figure 20) The diaphragm also serves as a fire and dust stop

There is no finish for iron or steel which is permanent It is therefore best to use for the fixed parts of a stack some coating such as paint or air drying enamel which can be renewed in place Baked enamel is very hard and tough at first and presents a good appearance, but it will gradually become abraded and worn through the general wear and tear of ordinary usage After a few years the color deadens and the enamel loses its life so that it chips and cracks, especially where applied on large surfaces It can then be renewed only by rubbing off what remains of the coating, dipping the parts again and baking them in an oven at a high temperature. This process is impossible for the fixed parts and can be employed for the shelves alone.

The standard cast iron shelf supports have been tested by the Ordnance Department of the United States Government at the Watertown Arsenal, Mass, and found amply strong to carry their loads

BOOK STACK AND SHELVING FOR LIBRARIES

THE SNEAD AND COMPANY IRON WORKS

DOUBLE FACED RANGE OF SIX COMPARTMENTS
(Figure 25)

THE general description given for figure 24 applies as well here, the construction of the ranges being identical and only the design of the range front changing

It should be noted that the diagonal braces shown in figure 25 are not required where the range is attached to the wall or is connected at the top to the floor framing of an upper tier

BOOK STACK AND SHELVING FOR LIBRARIES

ALTERNATIVE DESIGN OF RANGE FOR 10″ SHELVES
(Figure 25)

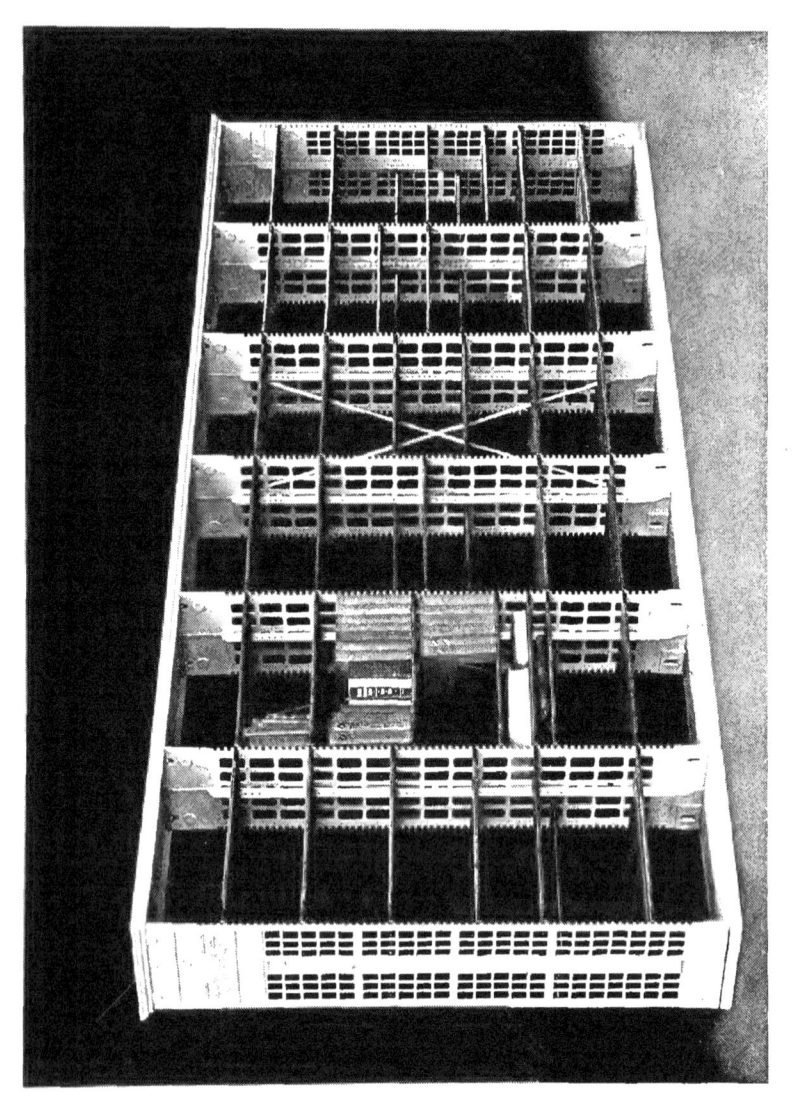

THE SNEAD AND COMPANY IRON WORKS

WALL RANGE
(Figure 26)

FOR single faced ranges placed against the walls the ends are designed to harmonize with the double faced ranges, as will be seen by comparing figures 26 with figure 24

These cases are suitable for offices and private residences as well as for libraries

BOOK STACK AND SHELVING FOR LIBRARIES

THE SNEAD AND COMPANY IRON WORKS

ACCESSORIES

THE skeleton shelves and the openness of the construction of the Green-Snead Book Stack render feasible the use of many convenient accessories to meet the needs of library administration

The perforations in the range fronts can be used to attach hanging card frames as shown on the opposite page The shape, size and design of these may be varied to suit special requirements.

It is frequently found necessary to have some means of preventing books from being pushed back too far on a shelf The steel back stop shown serves this purpose as it can be secured by the keys through any of the slits in the shelf This stop causes the fronts of books of regular depth to form a straight line and present a good appearance, it prevents small books from being lost to view behind larger ones It is especially useful in an open shelf room as the public is liable to be careless in replacing books

The special angle book support shown is a variation from that illustrated on page 29, it is equally convenient, more easily cleaned and cheaper

BOOK STACK AND SHELVING FOR LIBRARIES

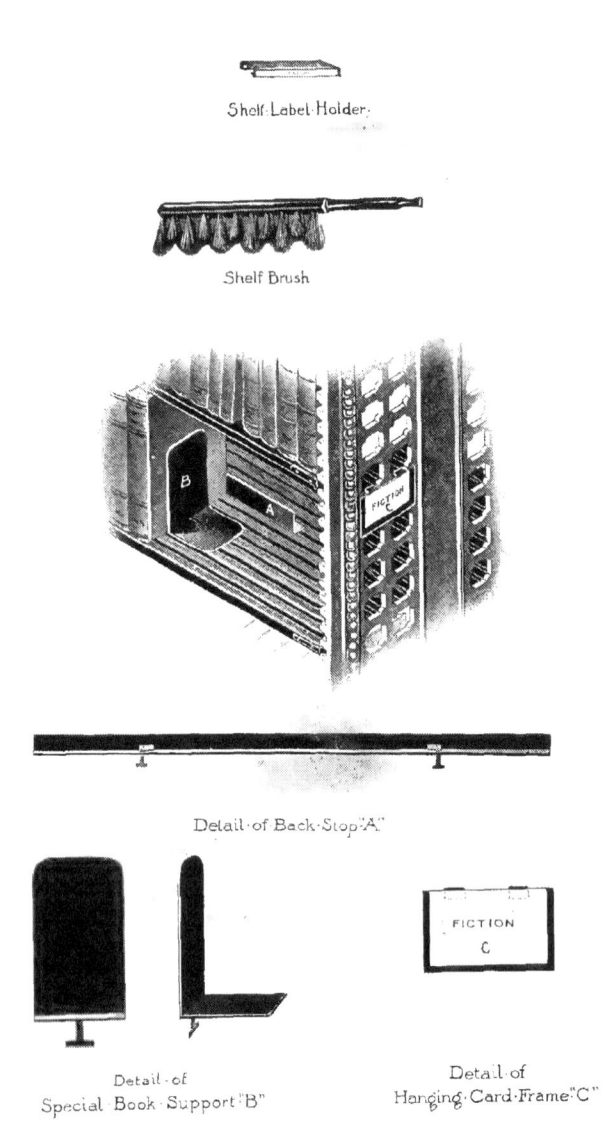

Shelf-Label-Holder

Shelf Brush

Detail of Back-Stop "A"

Detail of
Special Book Support "B"

Detail of
Hanging Card Frame "C"

THE SNEAD AND COMPANY IRON WORKS

CAST IRON BRACKET STACK
(Figures 27, 28 and 29)

THE bracket stack has been introduced to meet the wants of libraries where it is desired to have the shelves in each compartment of varying widths from bottom to top, or where the funds available for the purchase of stacks are limited

In designing this type of bracket stack an effort was made to carry out as far as possible the same principles which were followed for our standard stack   The result has been to make a bracket stack far superior to any other. The shelf supports are of solid cast iron, wasting no space and avoiding any hollow inaccessible places where dust can collect or rust form   Each shelf consists of a cold rolled steel plate, flanged at the front and back, on which side brackets are bolted   A unique design has been adopted for the brackets so that when secured in place they are perfectly rigid and will always fit the supports   The front edge of each bracket is flanged to prevent it from entering between the leaves of a book and causing injury   This obviates a serious fault common to nearly every bracket stack.

Figure 29 shows the shelves with perforated cast iron brackets. Shelves may be of wood

STEEL BRACKET STACK
(Figures 30 and 31)

A more economical bracket stack than the cast iron type is the construction shown in Figures 30 and 31   The stack and shelves throughout are made exclusively of steel

There is practically no loss of book storage space between adjoining compartments and the shelves are more easily adjusted and not so easily dislodged as in the bracket stacks of other makes   Each shelf bracket is supported on the upright at five points simultaneously   The shelves are similar in construction to those described above for the cast iron bracket stack

ORNAMENTAL ENDS
(Figures 32 and 33)

Where a bracket stack is installed for reasons of economy it is frequently desired that it present the appearance of a standard stack from an end view   This is attained by the use of a "closed end" which hides the books and shelves   Figure 33 shows a "closed end" of cast iron   The design and ornament of this may be varied to suit the taste of the architect or librarian

Plainer ends can be furnished in cold rolled sheet steel.

Pilaster ends as shown in Figure 32 may be used for either the cast iron or steel bracket stacks

BOOK STACK AND SHELVING FOR LIBRARIES

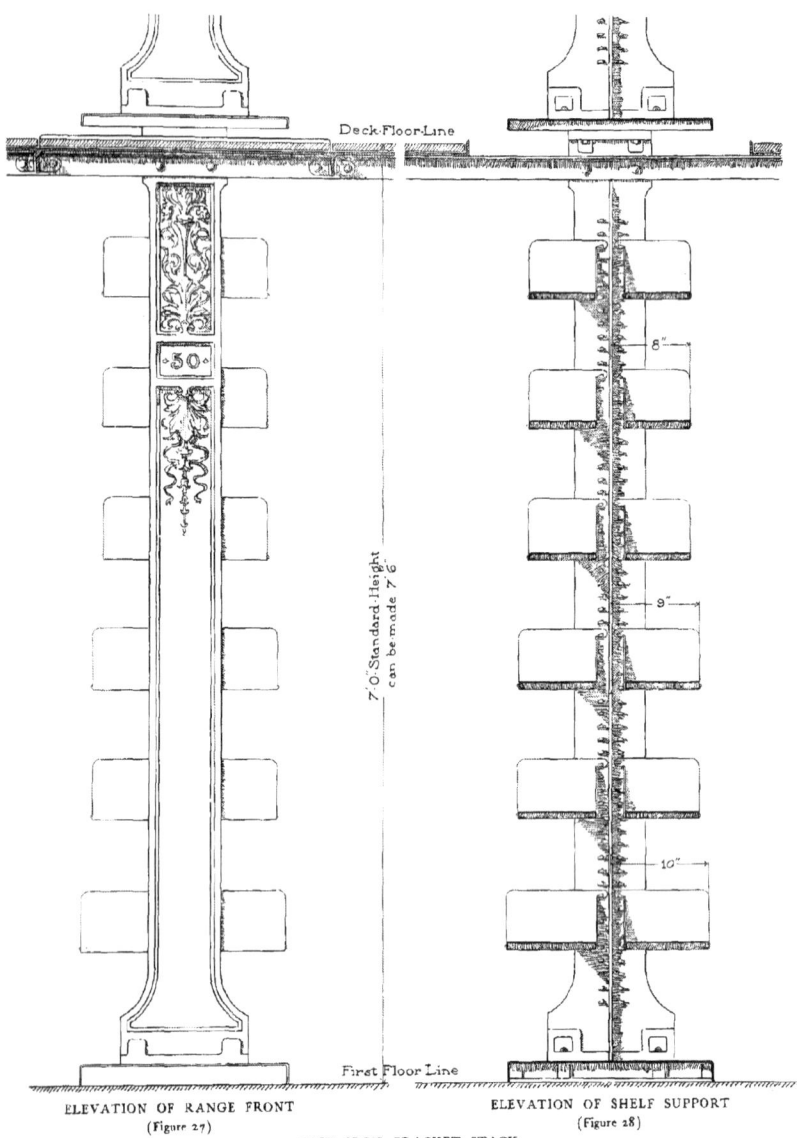

ELEVATION OF RANGE FRONT
(Figure 27)

ELEVATION OF SHELF SUPPORT
(Figure 28)

CAST IRON BRACKET STACK

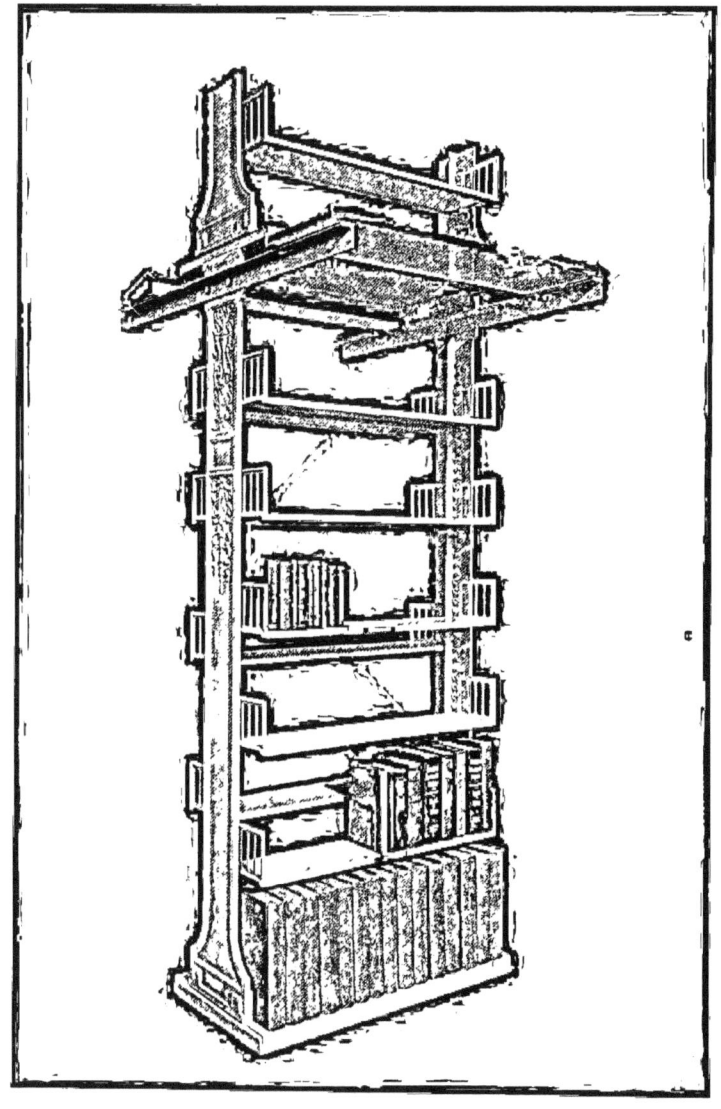

THE SNEAD AND COMPANY IRON WORKS

CAST IRON BRACKET STACK
(Figure 29)

BOOK STACK AND SHELVING FOR LIBRARIES

ELEVATION OF RANGE FRONT
(Figure 30)

STEEL BRACKET STACK

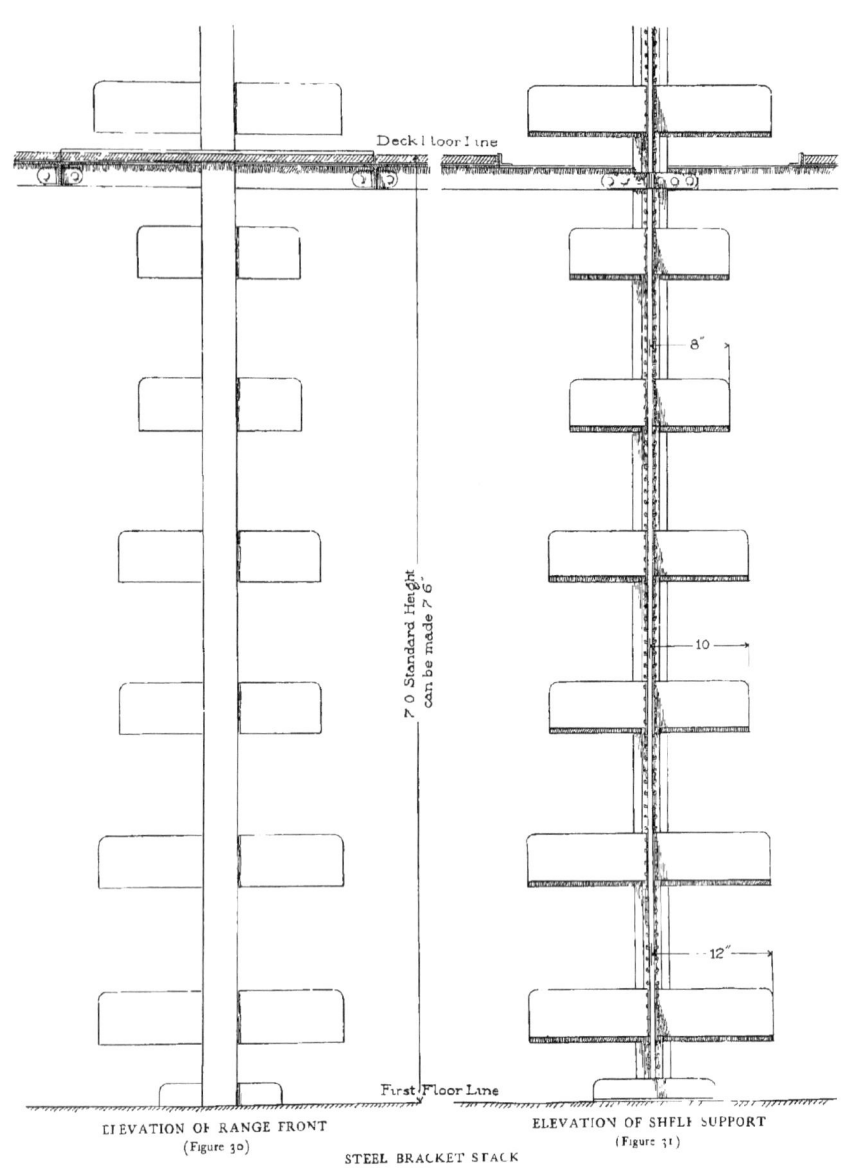

ELEVATION OF SHELF SUPPORT
(Figure 31)

THE SNEAD AND COMPANY IRON WORKS

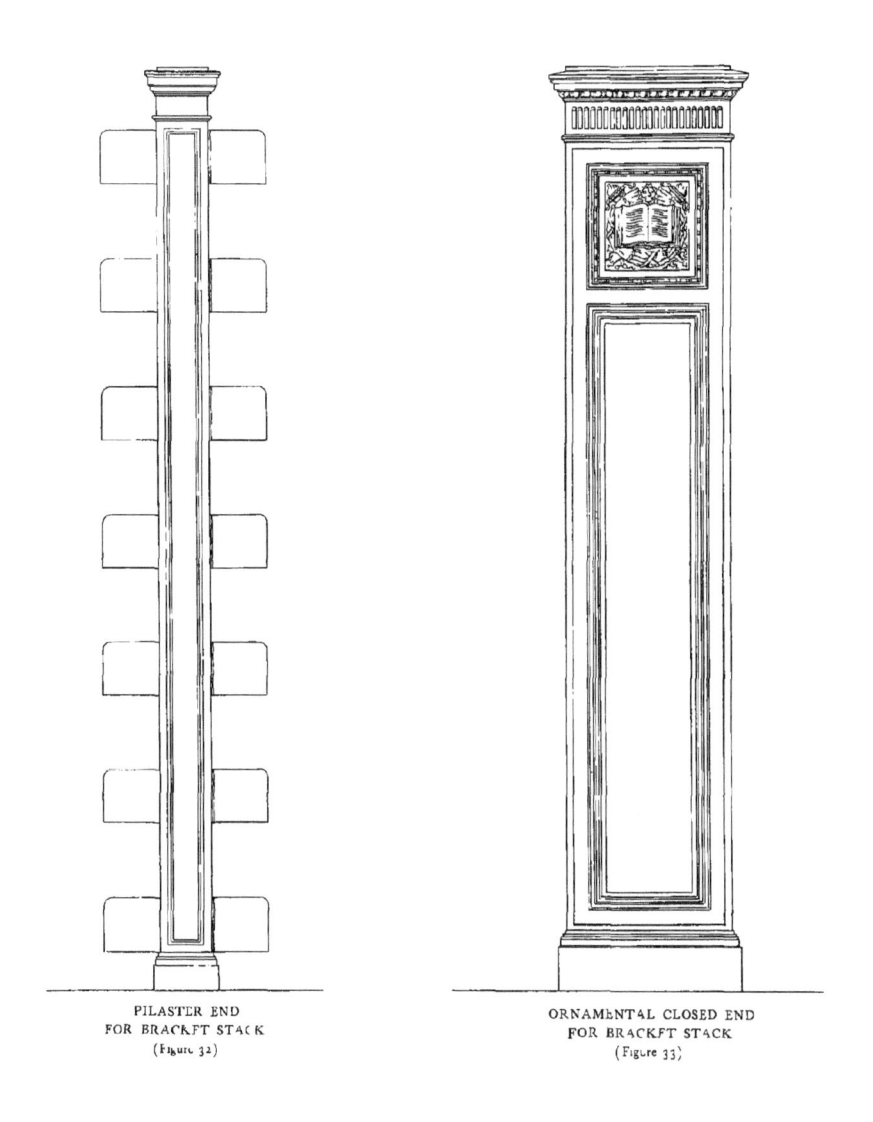

PILASTER END
FOR BRACKET STACK
(Figure 32)

ORNAMENTAL CLOSED END
FOR BRACKET STACK
(Figure 33)

BOOK STACK AND SHELVING FOR LIBRARIES

CAPACITY OF SHELVING

IN ascertaining the quantity of shelving required to accommodate a certain number of books the character of the library must be duly considered

For a law library but five volumes per running foot of shelf can be taken, for a scientific library seven volumes per foot, for a reference library eight volumes per foot and for a circulating public library ten volumes per foot

In stacks 7 or 7½-ft high, seven shelves (six adjustable and one fixed) are usually counted in each single-faced 3-ft shelf compartment

From the above data the following table is formulated

	Vols per running ft of shelf	Vols per single-faced 3-ft compartment	Vols per double-faced 3-f compartment
Law Library,	5	105	210
Scientific Library,	7	147	294
Reference Library,	8	168	336
Circulating Library,	10	210	420

The question of depth of shelf to be adopted must also be determined from the books to be shelved In law and circulating public libraries an 8-in shelf is widely used, for a reference library several widths should be provided and for scientific collections the shelves are best 11 or 12 inches deep

It is of importance when comparing prices of different types of stacks to also compare their relative capacities The amount of space available for storing books is not determined by the total length of each range multiplied by the number of shelves in each compartment, but by the net length of each shelf, found by measuring the clear distance between supports, multiplied by the total number of shelves

THE SNEAD AND COMPANY IRON WORKS

TABLE OF WEIGHTS OF BOOK STACKS AND DECK FLOORS

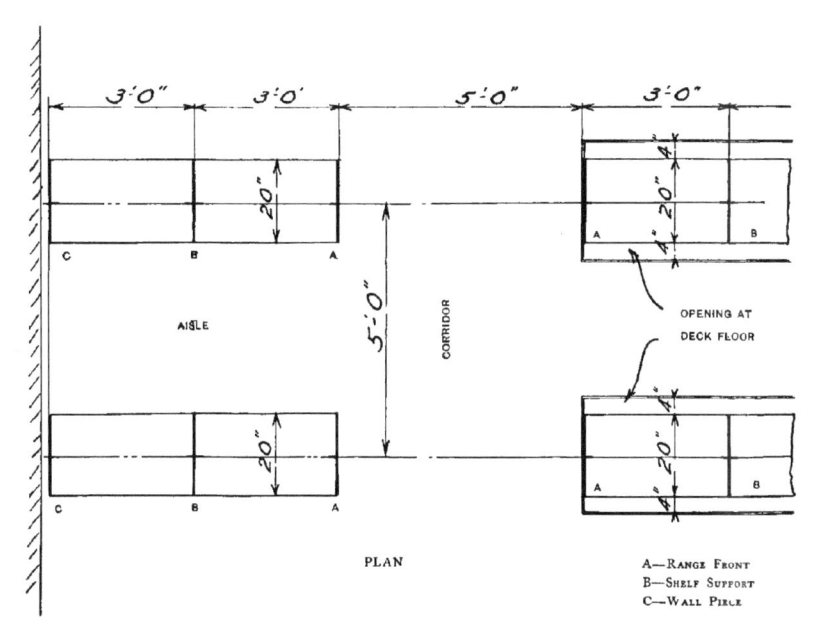

AVERAGED WEIGHTS

Deck Floor Framing—6 lbs per sq ft Gross Area
¾" Glass Flooring—10 lbs per sq ft Net Area
1½" Marble Flooring—20 lbs per sq ft Net Area.
Stacks and Shelves—10 lbs per cu ft of Stack
Books—20 lbs per cu ft of Stack

Live load taken at 40 lbs per square foot net area for top floor and reduced ten per cent for each floor below

For Tables of Loads see pages 67 and 68

TABLE OF LOADS
USING ¾" GLASS FLOORING

TIER	LOADS IN LBS	A	B	C
12th,	Dead, Live,	770 660	1,190 320	595 160
11th,	Total from above, Dead, Live,	1,430 770 595	1,510 1,190 290	755 595 145
10th,	Total, Dead, Live,	2,795 770 535	2,990 1,190 260	1,495 595 130
9th,	Total, Dead, Live,	4,100 770 480	4,440 1,190 240	2,220 595 120
8th,	Total, Dead, Live,	5,350 770 435	5,870 1,190 210	2,935 595 105
7th,	Total, Dead, Live,	6,555 770 390	7,270 1,190 190	3,635 595 95
6th,	Total, Dead, Live,	7,715 770 350	8,650 1,190 170	4,325 595 85
5th,	Total, Dead, Live,	8,835 770 315	10,010 1,190 150	5,005 595 75
4th,	Total, Dead, Live,	9,920 770 285	11,350 1,190 140	5,675 595 70
3d,	Total, Dead, Live,	10,975 770 255	12,680 1,190 130	6,340 595 65
2d,	Total, Dead, Live,	12,000 770 230	14,000 1,190 110	7,000 595 55
1st,	Total,	13,000	15,300	7,650

THE SNEAD AND COMPANY IRON WORKS

TABLE OF LOADS
USING 1½" MARBLE FLOORING

TIER	LOADS IN LBS	A	B	C
12th,	Dead,	940	1,270	635
	Live,	660	320	160
11th,	Total from above,	1,600	1,590	795
	Dead,	940	1,270	635
	Live,	595	290	145
10th,	Total,	3,135	3,150	1,575
	Dead,	940	1,270	635
	Live,	535	260	130
9th,	Total,	4,610	4,680	2,340
	Dead,	940	1,270	635
	Live,	480	240	120
8th,	Total,	6,030	6,190	3,095
	Dead,	940	1,270	635
	Live, .	435	210	105
7th,	Total,	7,405	7,670	3,835
	Dead,	940	1,270	635
	Live,	390	190	95
6th,	Total,	8,735	9,130	4,565
	Dead,	940	1,270	635
	Live,	350	170	85
5th	Total,	10,025	10,570	5,285
	Dead,	940	1,270	635
	Live,	315	150	75
4th,	Total,	11,280	11,990	5,995
	Dead,	940	1,270	635
	Live,	285	140	70
3d,	Total,	12,505	13,400	6,700
	Dead,	940	1,270	635
	Live,	255	130	65
2d,	Total,	13,700	14,800	7,400
	Dead,	940	1,270	635
	Live,	230	110	55
1st,	Total,	14,870	16,180	8,090

BOOK STACK AND SHELVING FOR LIBRARIES

ELECTRIC LIGHTING

EVERY stack room, whether provided with windows or surrounded by blank walls, is dependent at times upon artificial illumination and this should be provided only by means of incandescent electric lamps placed in the ceiling of the stack aisles and corridors, the conduits containing the wires being supported directly by the deck framing

The distribution of light and method of control may be varied to suit the individual requirements, the lights, however should be not more than six feet apart in the stack aisles and from twelve to fourteen feet apart in the corridors

For separate control of the lights in each stack aisle between the ranges switches may be placed on the stack ends, the vertical conduits or risers being enclosed in iron ducts, or a hanging tassel switch can be used   The latter form answers every purpose and is the more economical because of not requiring the vertical conduits or ducts   It has the further advantage of leaving all the wiring and switches easily accessible for alteration or repair   For a stack room open to readers it is best to have the lights controlled individually by means of a key or chain pull

In the large libraries, notably the Library of Congress and the New York Public Library, each stack floor is divided into several sections and all of the wires brought to central points where switch boards are located to control the lighting of the respective sections   This greatly reduces the cost of installation and has the advantage of grouping the switches at convenient points where the library attendants pass regularly

THE SNEAD AND COMPANY IRON WORKS

BOOK LIFTS

FOR a small library with a stack of two or three tiers the vertical book lift is usually of the dumb-waiter type, the car being of wood or sheet steel two shelves high and operated by a hand rope. The upper shelf should be hinged at the back and arranged to drop down when large books are to be carried.

In a high stack the same style of car may be used but the power should be electric with automatic push button control. With this arrangement the car may be sent to or brought from any landing by pushing the proper button and it stops automatically at the desired landing. The doors in the enclosure of the book lift shaft are equipped with automatic switches which prevent the starting of the car until all doors are closed. The electric lifts generally operate with a speed of from 100 to 150 feet per minute with a capacity of from 100 to 300 pounds.

When it is necessary to convey the books horizontally from one part of the building to another mechanical carriers are employed and these can be designed to serve as both carrier and lift operating as an endless chain.

BOOK STACK AND SHELVING FOR LIBRARIES

THE LIBRARY OF CONGRESS
WASHINGTON, D C
SMITHMEYER & PELZ AND EDWARD P CASEY, Architects

THE SNEAD AND COMPANY IRON WORKS

LIBRARY OF CONGRESS, WASHINGTON, D. C.

SMITHMEYER & PELZ AND EDWARD P CASEY, Architects

AN Act of Congress, passed April 15, 1886, authorized the construction of a library building substantially according to the plan submitted by John L Smithmeyer in the Italian renaissance style of architecture, with such modifications as might be found necessary or advantageous

The original designs for the building were furnished by John L Smithmeyer and Paul J Pelz and the architectural details were worked out by Paul J Pelz and Edward P Casey The construction of the building was under the direction of a commission until October, 1888, when, before the foundations were laid, the commission was abolished by Congress and the work placed under the control of General Thomas L Casey, the Chief of Engineers of the Army, with directions to submit a plan for approval   He placed Bernard R Green in charge as superintendent and engineer, who, upon the death of General Casey, March 25, 1896, succeeded to full control until the building was completed February 28, 1897, at the cost of $6,344,585 34, exclusive of the land

The building is approximately 470 feet by 340 feet with four inner courts 150 feet by 75 feet to 100 feet, and consists of cellar, basement, first, second and attic stories, with an octagonal dome rising 120 feet above the main roof It has 32,600 square feet, or nearly eight acres of floor space

The central feature is the main reading room, 100 feet in diameter, extending from the first floor 125 feet to the inner dome and lighted through eight large arched windows in the clerestory It has 210 desks and 36 alcove tables and can accommodate 250 readers at one time In the alcoves there are two stories of metal shelving holding over 120,000 volumes The issue desk is in the center of the reading room, it is connected with the three stacks by pneumatic tubes and with the two main stacks with mechanical book carriers

Each stack has nine "decks" or floors, seven feet from floor to floor The dimensions and capacities of the stacks are as follows

North Stack, 44' 8" x 110' 0" x 65' 0" high—capacity,	713,500	volumes
South Stack, 44' 8" x 110' 0" x 65' 0" " "	713,500	"
East Stack, 44' 8" x 30' 0" x 65' 0" " "	173,000	"
Total capacity,	1,600,000	volumes

BOOK STACK AND SHELVING FOR LIBRARIES

The first story also contains the senators' reading room and the representatives' reading room, besides rooms set apart for periodicals, maps and charts, bibliography, cataloguing, order division, general administration and the librarian

The divisions of manuscripts, documents, prints, exhibits of books, manuscripts and prints, and the Smithsonian division are located in the second story. The Smithsonian room is 131 feet long by 35 feet wide and has a book stack of three decks with capacity of about 150,000 volumes, provided with an electric elevator

A three tier stack has also been installed in the north curtain, second floor, for manuscripts and documents, the total capacity being 250,000 volumes. The westerly stacks in the first tier are enclosed with plate glass for greater security

The building already contains some 56 miles of shelving for books not inclusive of that for prints, music and maps and charts

In the attic are rooms for photography, repair of prints and manuscripts, storage, a public restaurant, and a room containing a book stack of 80,000 volumes capacity for the Slavic section

Outside of the three main stacks the basement story contains the reading room for the blind, the departments of music and copyrights, a branch of the Government Printing Office, the offices of the superintendent, chief clerk and the watch, and the mail room which handles all material arriving at or dispatched from the library building, including all mail matter and books delivered for outside use

The cellar space is devoted to the machinery room, heating apparatus, workshops and storage. The boilers and coal vaults are located under the parking, near but quite outside the building at the east front

THE SNEAD AND COMPANY IRON WORKS

LIBRARY OF CONGRESS, WASHINGTON, D. C.
SMITHMEYER & PELZ AND EDWARD P. CASEY, ARCHITECTS

BOOK STACK AND SHELVING FOR LIBRARIES

LIBRARY OF CONGRESS WASHINGTON, D C — FIRST FLOOR PLAN
SMITHMEYER & PELZ AND EDWARD P CASEY ARCHITECTS

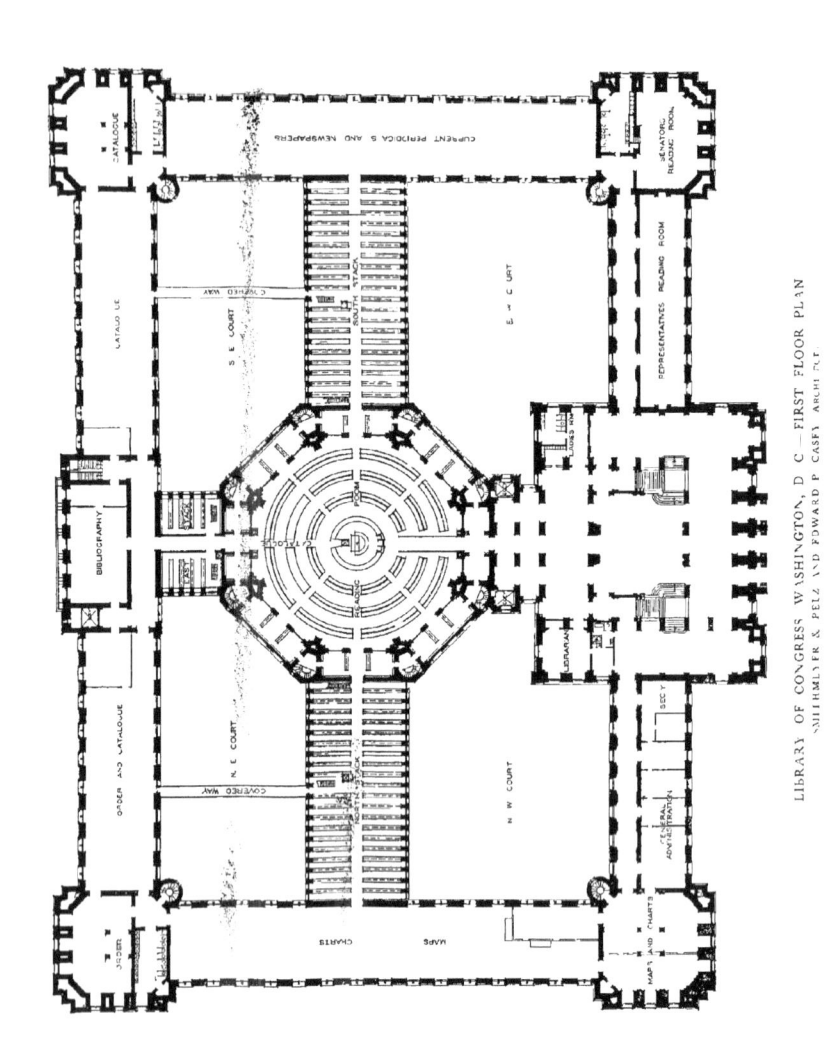

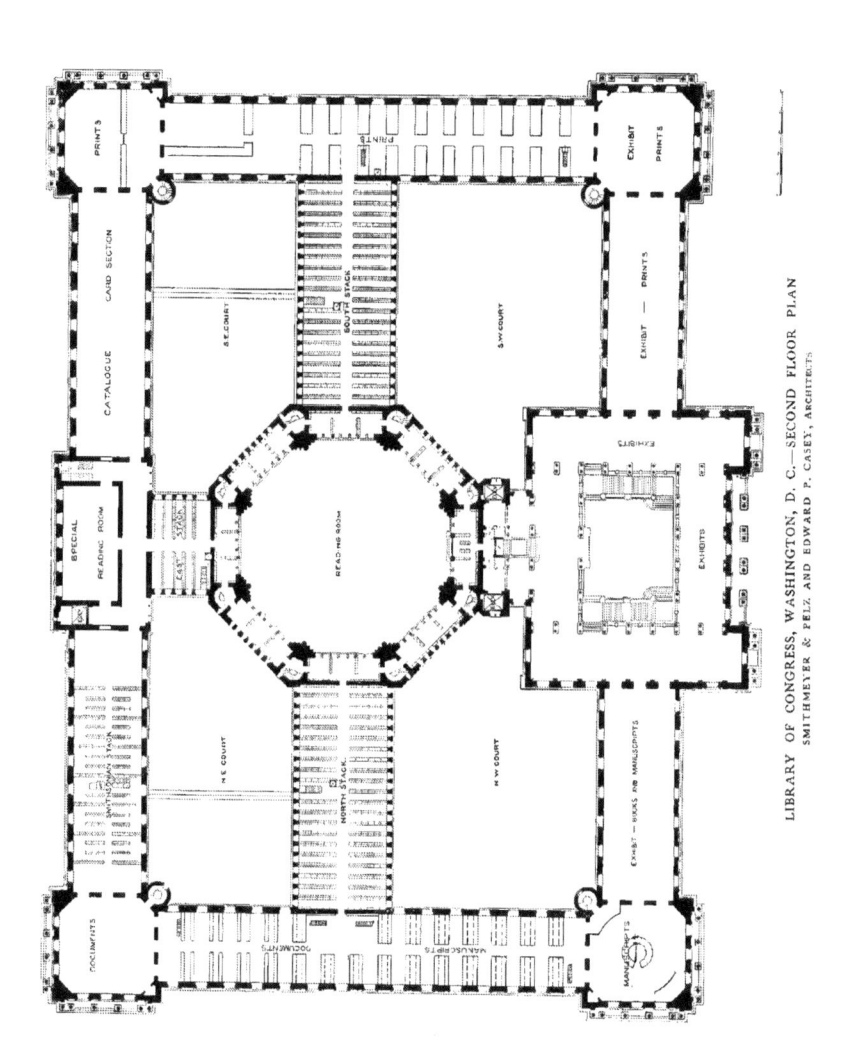

THE SNEAD AND COMPANY IRON WORKS

LIBRARY OF CONGRESS, WASHINGTON, D. C.—SECOND FLOOR PLAN
SMITHMEYER & PELZ AND EDWARD P. CASEY, ARCHITECTS

BOOK STACK AND SHELVING FOR LIBRARIES

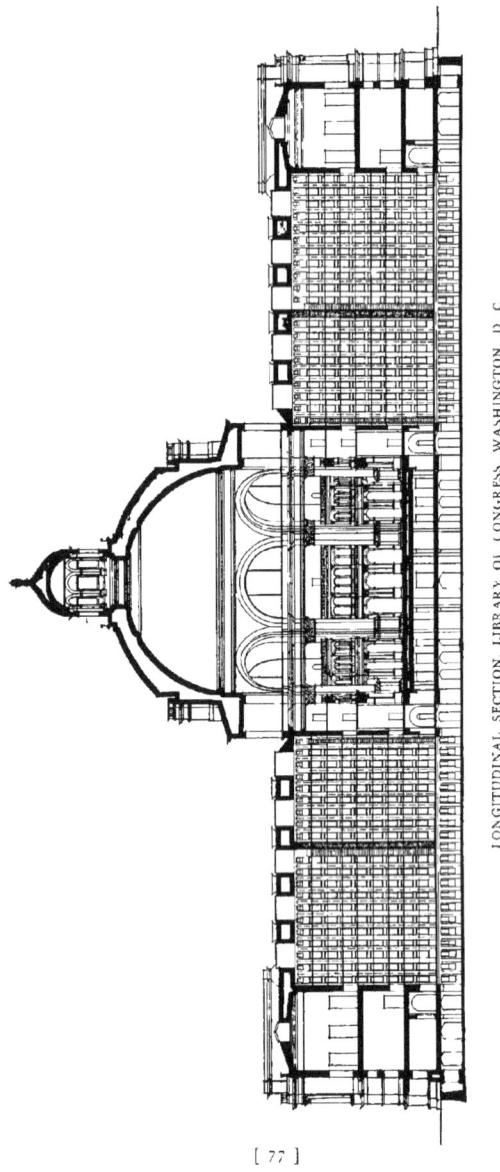

LONGITUDINAL SECTION, LIBRARY OF CONGRESS, WASHINGTON D C
SMITHMEYER & PELZ AND EDWARD P CASEY ARCHITECTS

THE SNEAD AND COMPANY IRON WORKS

THE MAIN READING ROOM, LIBRARY OF CONGRESS, WASHINGTON, D. C.
SMITHMEYER & PELZ AND EDWARD P. CASEY, ARCHITECTS

BOOK STACK AND SHELVING FOR LIBRARIES

VIEW AT STAIRWAY IN THE NORTH STACK, LIBRARY OF CONGRESS, WASHINGTON, D. C.
SMITHMEYER & PELZ AND EDWARD P. CASEY, Architects

THE SNEAD AND COMPANY IRON WORKS

EXTERIOR OF THE NORTH STACK, LIBRARY OF CONGRESS, WASHINGTON, D. C.
SMITHMEYER & PELZ AND EDWARD P. CASEY, ARCHITECTS

BOOK STACK AND SHELVING FOR LIBRARIES

A FLOOR IN THE NORTH STACK, LIBRARY OF CONGRESS, WASHINGTON, D. C.
SMITHMEYER & PELZ AND EDWARD P. CASEY, ARCHITECTS

BOOK STACK AND SHELVING FOR LIBRARIES

THE NEW YORK PUBLIC LIBRARY
NEW YORK CITY
CARRERE & HASTINGS, Architects

THE SNEAD AND COMPANY IRON WORKS

NEW YORK PUBLIC LIBRARY
CARRÈRE & HASTINGS, Architects

THE New York Public Library was founded on the 23d of May, 1895, by the consolidation of the Astor Library, Lenox Library and the Tilden Trust, a board of twenty-one trustees being elected from the boards of these three corporations. Provision was made for maintaining a free public library, with such branches as might be considered advisable.

The site chosen for the main building was in Bryant Park on Fifth Avenue between 40th and 42d streets, at the easterly end then occupied by the old reservoir. The Legislature passed a law in May, 1896, authorizing the removal of the reservoir and the lease of the land to the Library, and a year later an act was passed providing for the construction by the city of a library building on this site.

On November 11, 1897, the architects were selected in competition for the new building and in December the plans were approved by the city. The removal of the reservoir was begun in June, 1899, and the entire building was under roof at the end of November, 1906. Since that time the construction has progressed as rapidly as possible with a structure of this monumental character and it is expected that the building will be completed by 1911 at a total cost of over $7,000,000.00.

The general dimensions of the building are 390 feet front by 270 feet deep and the heights of the floors are as follows — cellar, 13 feet, basement, 15 feet, first story, 22 feet 6 inches, second story, 16 feet, third story, ceiling height 11 to 23 feet, main reading room, 50 feet. The area covered by the library exclusive of the open south court, is 115,000 square feet. The north court is enclosed under a glass roof. The total floor space, exclusive of the cellar, is nearly nine acres.

The basement is the main floor of the building so far as the business of the library is concerned. It contains the lending delivery room entered directly by the entrance to the north. Along the front to the south and extending down the side to the driveway entering the south court are the book binding department and printing office. Across the corridor from the front is a lunch room for library employees.

The principal entrance to the first floor gives direct access to the rotunda. At the right as one enters is the technical science reading room. Across the corridor are the reading room for the blind, the elevator hall and lobby. Toward the rear on this side are two small reading rooms, and back of them is a large room devoted to patents

[84]

BOOK STACK AND SHELVING FOR LIBRARIES

At the left of the rotunda in the first story is the periodical room occupying the entire corner. Opposite this are several small rooms, among them a reception room.

The south side of this floor is given up to the administration of the library and there are the offices of the superintendent, the working room of the clerks, the office of the chief of circulation, and a receiving and checking room.

The second story, as can be seen on the plan, contains rooms for applied science, economics and documents, the Hebrew room and the Russian room, the director's and trustee's rooms, and space for a series of small studies, the order, cataloguing and accessions rooms.

On the third floor, in a large room over the rotunda in the center of the front, will be the Stuart collection of rare works. Other rooms on this floor are for music, photography, art and architecture, prints, manuscripts, maps, picture galleries and reading rooms.

The main bookstack occupies the larger part of the rear of the building and extends upward through the basement, first and second stories. It is 297 feet long, 78 feet wide, and is made up of seven tiers each 7 feet 6 inches high with marble floors. Each tier contains 978 double-faced compartments for 9-inch shelves and 146 compartments for 12-inch shelves. Along the walls are compartments 24 inches, 26 inches and 30 inches deep, fitted with sliding shelves. In all the main stack contains 96,000 adjustable and 16,000 fixed shelves, which, placed end to end, would extend a distance of 63 miles, the capacity of this big stack is 3,200,000 volumes. In 53 other rooms in the basement, first, second and third stories metal bookstacks are provided with a combined capacity of 900,000 volumes, making the building's total capacity over 4,000,000 books.

On the third floor immediately above the main stack and carried by it is the main reading room, 76 feet by 295 feet, capable of seating about 700 readers. The roof is high, rising above the main portion of the building, and the room is lighted by a series of windows on both sides of its entire length. In the center is the delivery department, the electric elevators and the pneumatic tubes connecting with the stack room below.

One of the features of this library is a vacuum sweeper system and this will be utilized in cleaning the books and stack room shelves, doing away with the old time microbe-scattering brushes and dust cloths.

THE SNEAD AND COMPANY IRON WORKS

PLASTER MODEL OF NEW YORK PUBLIC LIBRARY
CARRÈRE & HASTINGS, ARCHITECTS

BOOK STACK AND SHELVING FOR LIBRARIES

FRONT ELEVATION, NEW YORK PUBLIC LIBRARY
CARRÈRE & HASTINGS, ARCHITECTS

THE SNEAD AND COMPANY IRON WORKS

REAR ELEVATION SHOWING STACK ROOM WINDOWS, NEW YORK PUBLIC LIBRARY
CARRÈRE & HASTINGS, ARCHITECTS

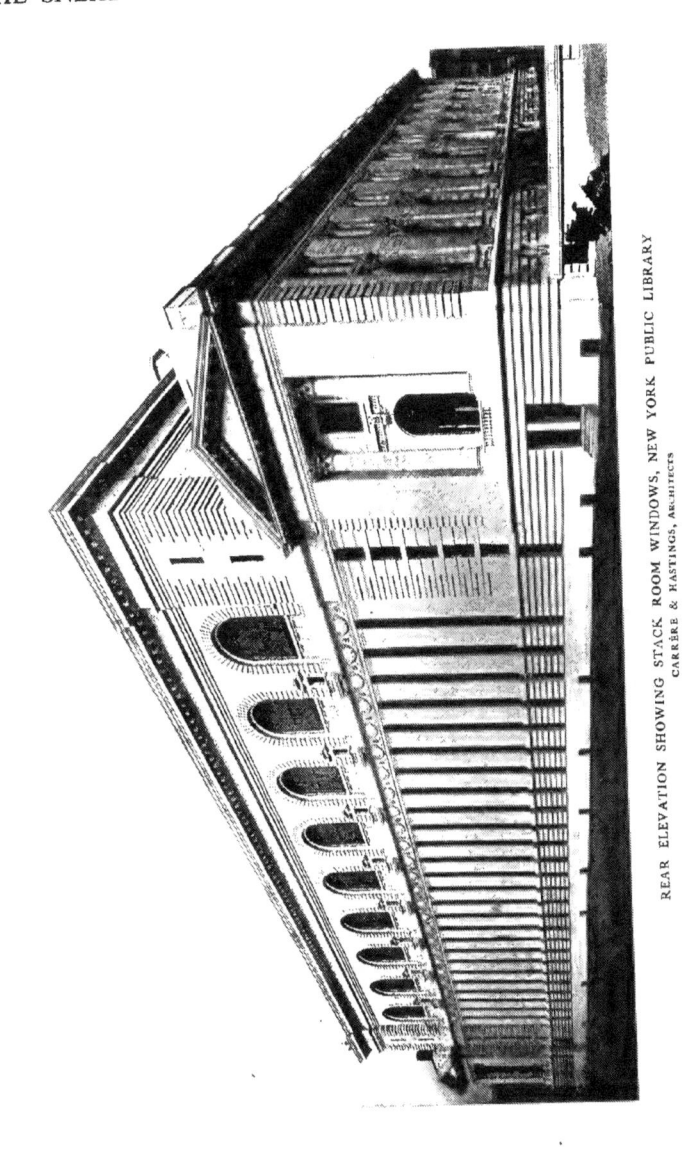

BOOK STACK AND SHELVING FOR LIBRARIES

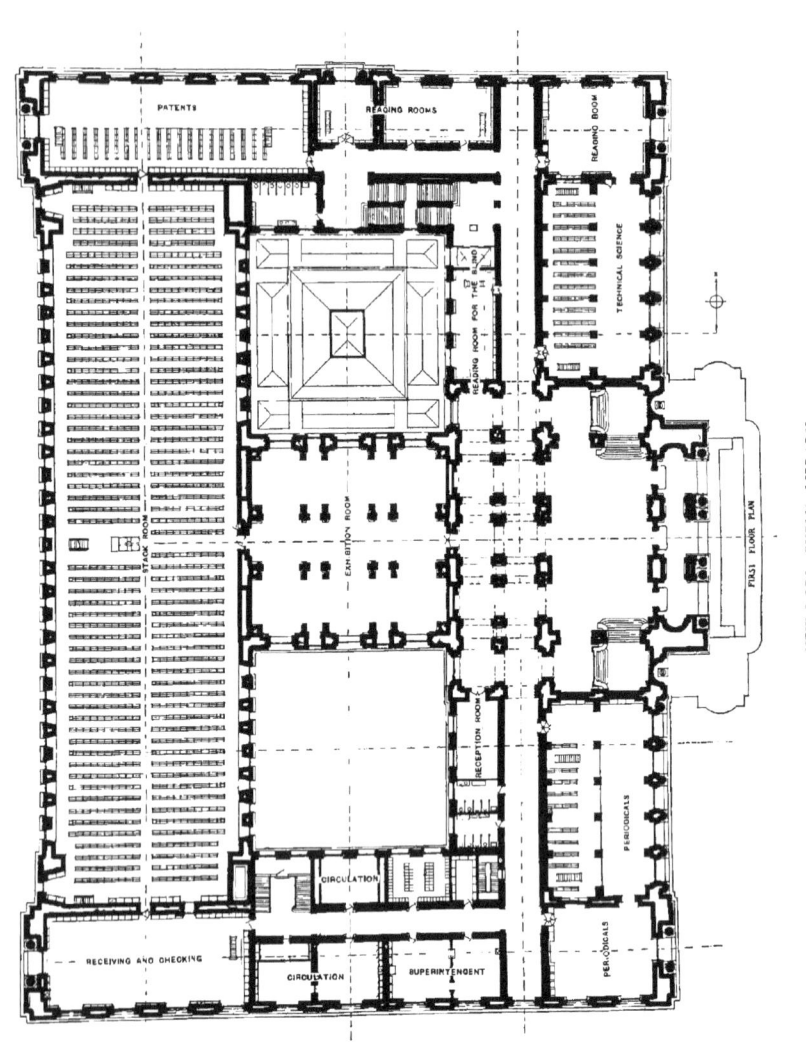

NEW YORK PUBLIC LIBRARY
CARRÈRE & HASTINGS, ARCHITECTS
FIRST FLOOR PLAN

THE SNEAD AND COMPANY IRON WORKS

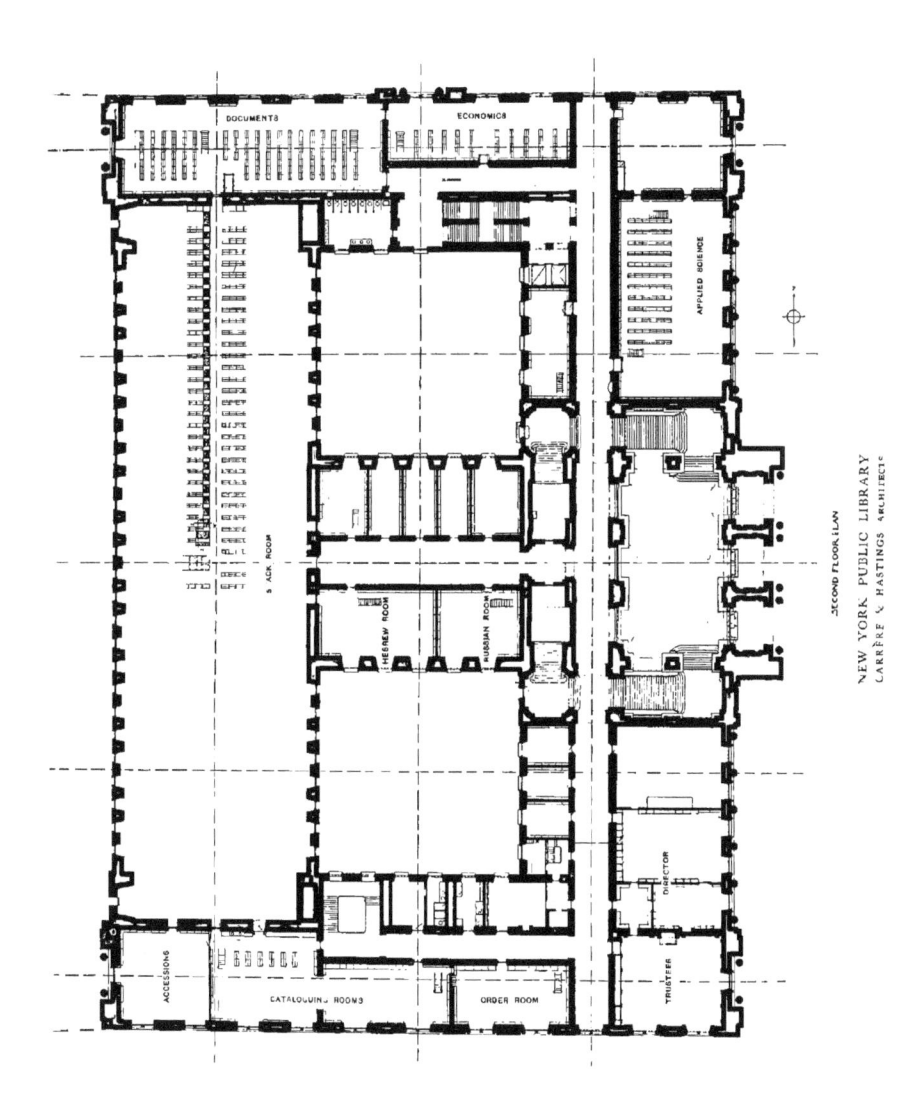

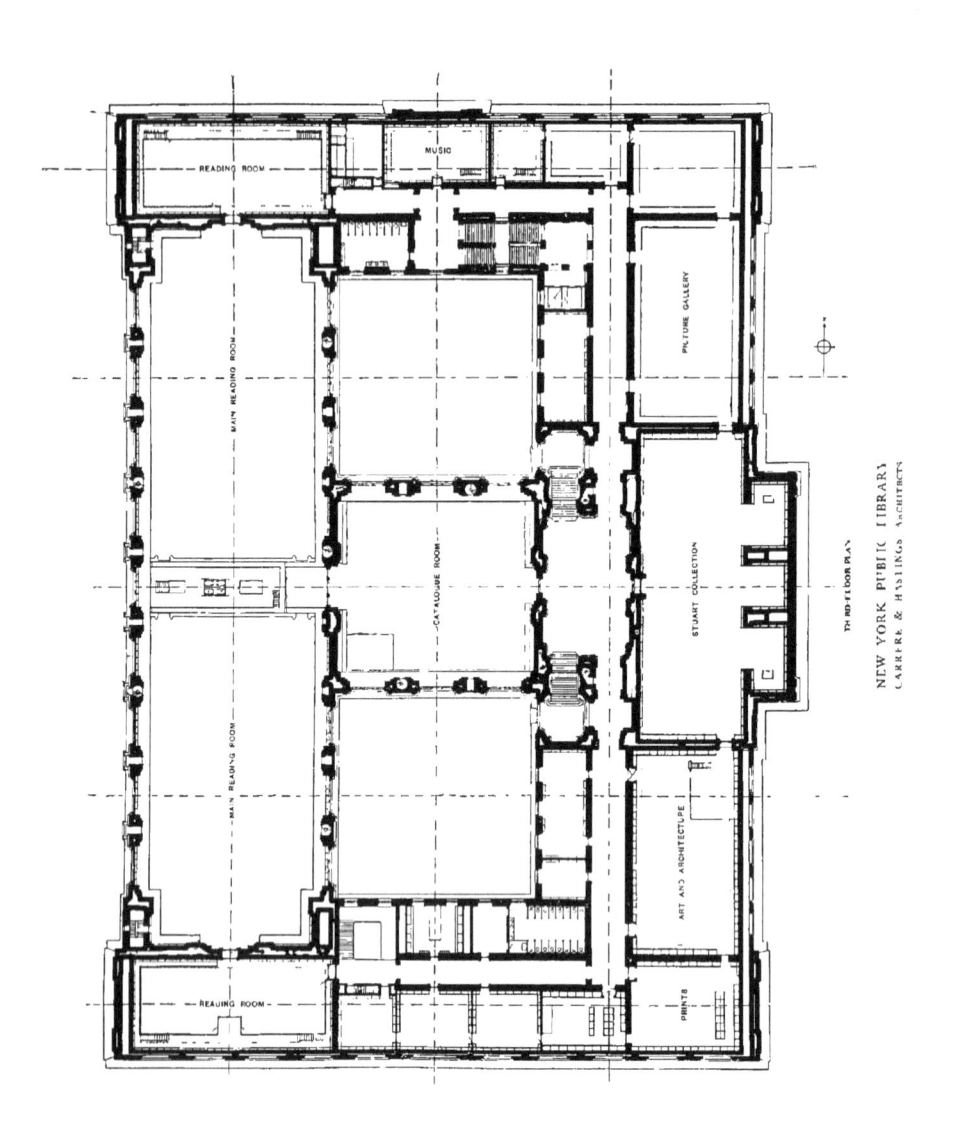

BOOK STACK AND SHELVING FOR LIBRARIES

THE SNEAD AND COMPANY IRON WORKS

THE STACK FRAME IN PROCESS OF ERECTION, NEW YORK PUBLIC LIBRARY
CARRÈRE & HASTINGS, ARCHITECTS

BOOK STACK AND SHELVING FOR LIBRARIES

STACK FRAME IN SEVENTH TIER, SUPPORTING READING-ROOM FLOOR ABOVE THE STACK, NEW YORK PUBLIC LIBRARY
CARRÈRE & HASTINGS, Architects

THE SNEAD AND COMPANY IRON WORKS

FIRST TIER OF STACK, NEW YORK PUBLIC LIBRARY
(ALL FLOORS ARE TO BE COVERED WITH WHITE MARBLE)
CARRÈRE & HASTINGS, ARCHITECTS

BOOK STACK AND SHELVING FOR LIBRARIES

INTERMEDIATE TIER OF STACK, NEW YORK PUBLIC LIBRARY
(SHOWING VENTILATING DUCT ENCLOSED WITH CAST IRON PLATES)
CARRÈRE & HASTINGS, ARCHITECTS

THE SNEAD AND COMPANY IRON WORKS

MODEL OF STACK FOR NEW YORK PUBLIC LIBRARY
CARRÈRE & HASTINGS, Architects

BOOK STACK AND SHELVING FOR LIBRARIES

TYPICAL PLANS AND ILLUSTRATIONS OF

SMALLER LIBRARIES EQUIPPED WITH BOOK STACKS

MANUFACTURED AND INSTALLED BY

THE SNEAD AND COMPANY IRON WORKS

JERSEY CITY, N J.

BOOK STACK AND SHELVING FOR LIBRARIES

LOUISVILLE FREE PUBLIC LIBRARY, LOUISVILLE, KY.
PILCHER & TACHAU, ARCHITECTS

THE SNEAD AND COMPANY IRON WORKS

LOUISVILLE FREE PUBLIC LIBRARY
LOUISVILLE, KY.

PILCHER & TACHAU, Architects

THE general plan of this building is T-shaped with the entrance at the center, the public rooms in front, the stack room and office rooms in the rear in the base of the T

On the main floor the delivery desk is immediately in front, with a large reading room and reference room to the right, and an open shelf room to the left where 20,000 volumes will be accessible to the public Immediately back of the delivery desk is the stack room of five floors with a capacity of over 200,000 volumes, and around it in the basement and first stories are offices, order, cataloguing and supply rooms

On the second floor the left wing is occupied by the children's room and a small annex for teachers The right wing has class, study and art rooms There is a third story over the delivery room which will be used for museum purposes The two upper floors of the stack rise above the roof and are lighted directly through windows opposite each aisle

In the basement a lecture room with janitor and service rooms are located in the left wing, and in the right wing are rooms for newspapers and public documents Immediately under the delivery room is the fan, air-washing and other machinery This building is equipped with a vacuum cleaning system and in the stack room an electric elevator and book lift have been installed

The general outline of the building is conventional but the arrangement of the stack and work rooms is unique A very strong point is the compactness of the whole arrangement centering at the delivery desk, which makes it well adapted for work

BOOK STACK AND SHELVING FOR LIBRARIES

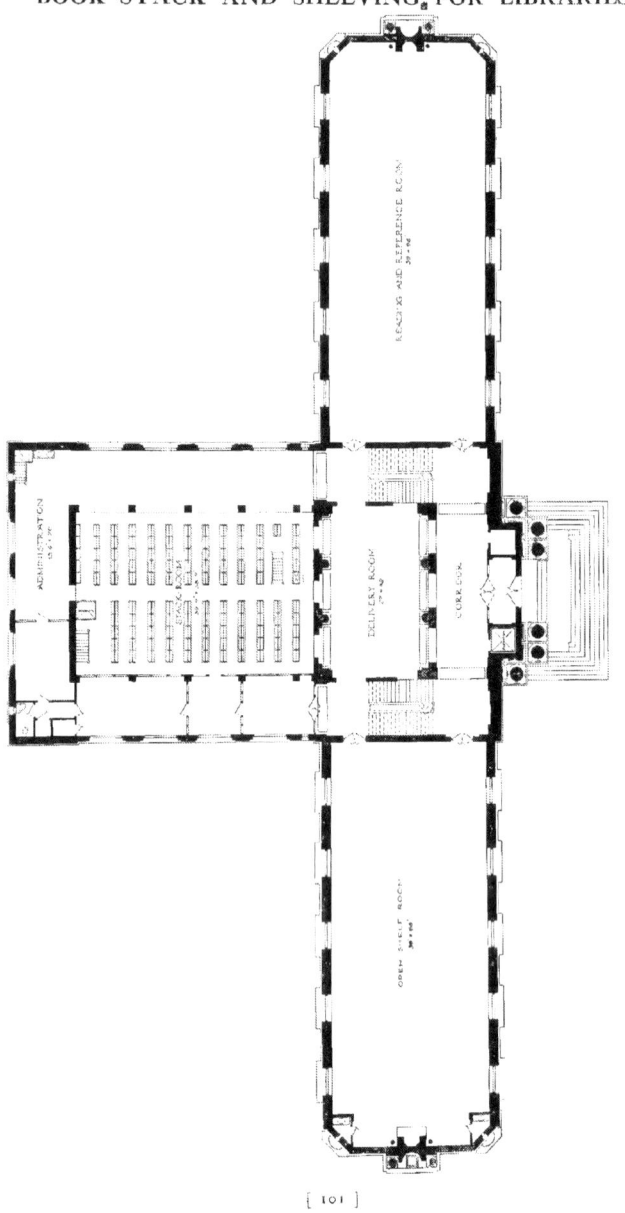

LOUISVILLE FREE PUBLIC LIBRARY, LOUISVILLE, KY
PILCHER & TACHAU, ARCHITECTS

THE SNEAD AND COMPANY IRON WORKS

LOUISVILLE FREE PUBLIC LIBRARY, LOUISVILLE, KY.
PILCHER & TACHAU, ARCHITECTS

BOOK STACK AND SHELVING FOR LIBRARIES

EVANSTON PUBLIC LIBRARY, EVANSTON, ILL.
JAS. GAMBLE ROGERS AND CHAS. A. PHILLIPS, ARCHITECTS

THE SNEAD AND COMPANY IRON WORKS

EVANSTON PUBLIC LIBRARY, EVANSTON, ILL.
JAS GAMBLE ROGERS AND CHAS A PHILLIPS, Architects

THE general dimensions of this building are 109 feet front by 90 feet in depth and the construction is fireproof throughout with the exception of the interior wood trim. The exterior is a beautiful example of simple classical design.

On the first floor the vestibule opens directly into the delivery hall beyond which are the loan desk and the stack room. At either side of the hall are the reading room and children's room, a view of each of these rooms being easily commanded from the loan desk.

The stack room extends to four stories in height, the basement tier is 11 ft 4 in. high, the next two tiers 7 ft 6 in., and the fourth tier 6 ft 6 in. high, with a total capacity of about 103,000 volumes. A skylight extends over nearly the entire area of this room.

The three walls of the stack room are laid up in a light buff colored face brick with all external angles rounded. The columns at the front of this room and all of the principal rooms in the first story are finished and furnished in mahogany.

Opening to the right of the stack room and connecting with the reading room is a large reference room 23 feet by 55 feet. At the left are the librarian's office and work rooms, and directly over them is the mezzanine story containing the directors' room, music room, the staff room and lavatory.

An audience or lecture room designed to accommodate about one hundred and fifty persons is provided in the basement, also a room for the use of the Evanston Historical Society, a room for boys and space for the janitor's quarters, men's lavatory, the heating and ventilating plant and the unpacking room.

BOOK STACK AND SHELVING FOR LIBRARIES

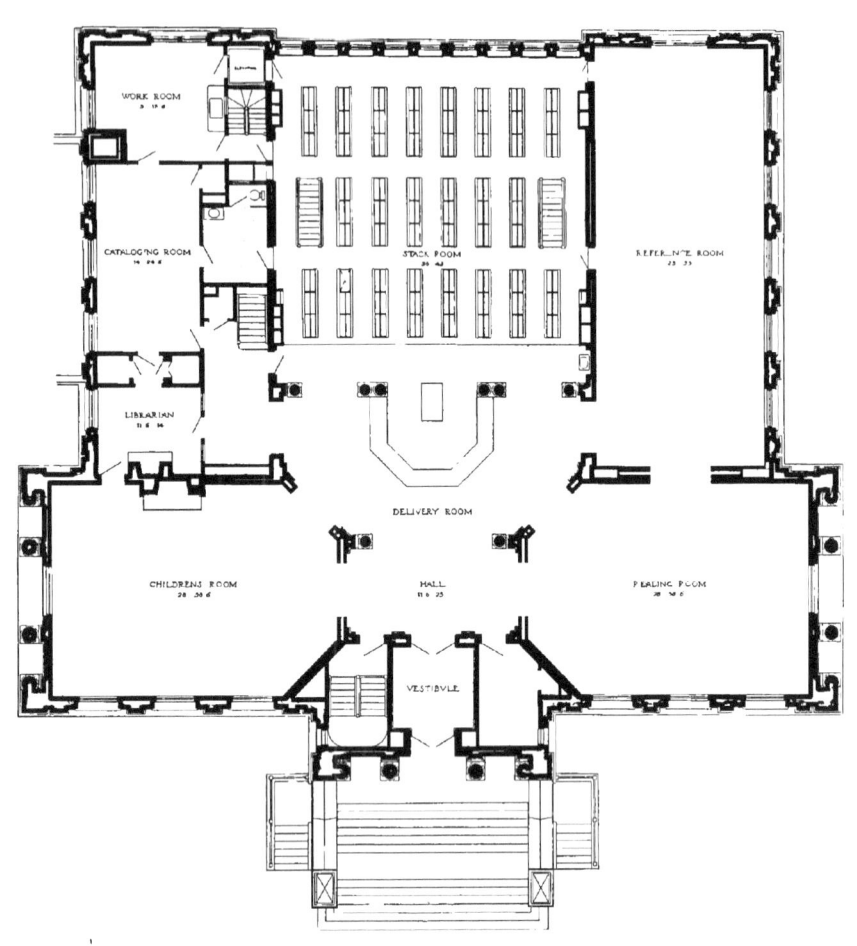

EVANSTON PUBLIC LIBRARY, EVANSTON, ILL
JAS GAMBLE ROGERS AND CHAS A PHILLIPS ARCHITECTS

THE SNEAD AND COMPANY IRON WORKS

EVANSTON PUBLIC LIBRARY, EVANSTON, ILL.
JAS. GAMBLE ROGERS AND CHAS. A. PHILLIPS, ARCHITECTS

BOOK STACK AND SHELVING FOR LIBRARIES

KRAUTH MEMORIAL LIBRARY, LUTHERAN THEOLOGICAL SEMINARY, MT. AIRY, PA.
WATSON & HUCKEL, Architects

THE SNEAD AND COMPANY IRON WORKS

KRAUTH MEMORIAL LIBRARY, LUTHERAN THEOLOGICAL SEMINARY, MT. AIRY, PHILADELPHIA, PA.
WATSON & HUCKEL, Architects

THE building consists of a central tower, two wings and a rear extension for the stack. The reading room, the central feature of the building, is about 35 feet square and 61 feet high, running through two stories to the roof, with an octagonal gallery at the second floor where are hung portraits, engravings, etc. This room is lighted by great upper windows and by a skylight.

The stack room is entirely fireproof, being separated from the rest of the building by a solid wall of masonry and "fire doors." There are three tiers of bookstacks, each 7½ feet in height, with glass floors between the stories; the total capacity of the stack is 98,000 volumes. The two rooms for the liturgical library and archives contain wall stacks 12 feet high with a capacity of 7,000 volumes.

The wing containing the auditorium is of one story. This room is for lectures and other purposes, finished in a churchly style and capable of seating 150 persons.

The other wing is of two stories above the basement, containing the periodical, librarian's and cataloguing rooms on the first floor, and a large seminar room and three research rooms on the second floor.

In the basement are found unpacking rooms, bindery, toilets and a large dining hall and kitchen.

BOOK STACK AND SHELVING FOR LIBRARIES

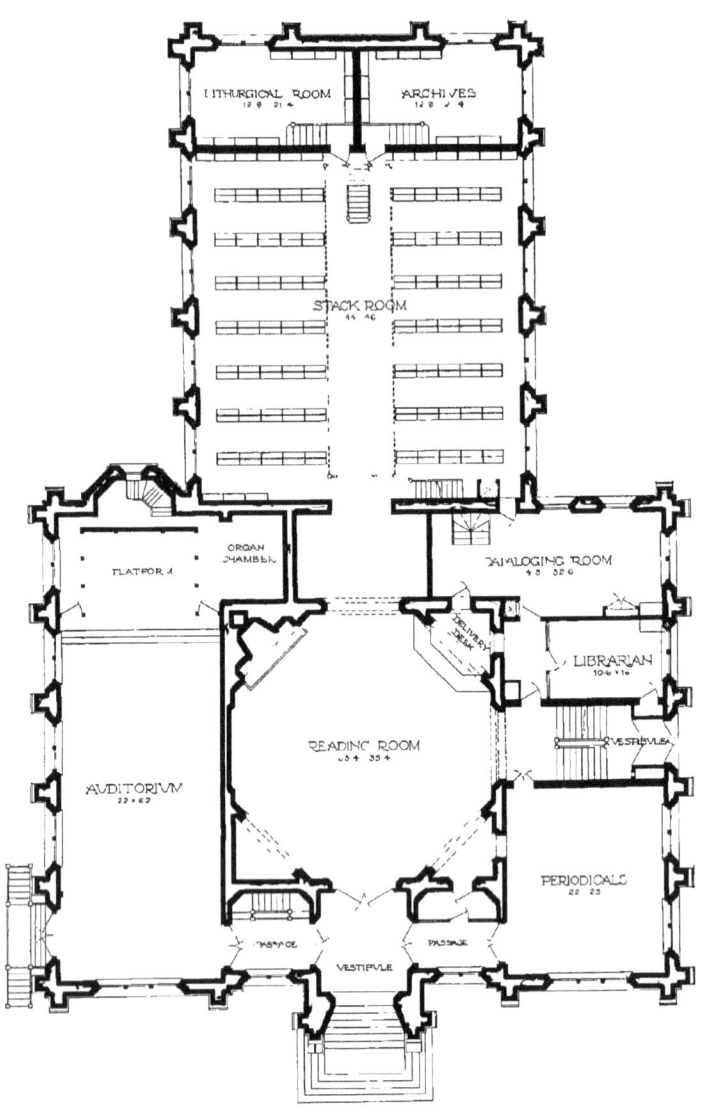

KRAUTH MEMORIAL LIBRARY, MT AIRY, PA
WATSON & HUCKEL, Architects

THE SNEAD AND COMPANY IRON WORKS

KRAUTH MEMORIAL LIBRARY, LUTHERAN THEOLOGICAL SEMINARY, MT. AIRY, PA.
WATSON & HUCKEL, ARCHITECTS

BOOK STACK AND SHELVING FOR LIBRARIES

BROOKLYN PUBLIC LIBRARY, WILLIAMSBURG BRANCH
WALKER & MORRIS, Architects

THE SNEAD AND COMPANY IRON WORKS

BROOKLYN PUBLIC LIBRARY, WILLIAMSBURG BRANCH, BROOKLYN, N. Y.

WALKER & MORRIS, Architects

THE Williamsburg Branch is the largest of the Brooklyn Branches of the Carnegie Library System and occupies a triangular site facing Division Avenue and bounded by Marcey Avenue and Rodney Street, thus securing exceptional lighting for all rooms

Taking advantage of the peculiarities of the site, the building has been so designed that the central delivery desk is the pivotal point Here the librarian has complete supervision of all this floor, including even the radial aisles in the stack room, at the same time the children s reading room and the main reading room are effectually separated from each other by the change in the direction of their axes

The stacks are in two tiers and the intermediate glass floor extends over the librarian's and staff locker rooms at a height of 7 ft 3 in above the main floor

The second story contains reading, reference, cataloguing, storage, librarian's and staff rooms

In the basement immediately under the main reading room is a lecture hall about 30 ft by 50 ft with stage, two anterooms and toilet The other basement wing contains work and storage rooms, and in the space underneath the stack room will be found toilets, boiler and fan rooms and coal storage

The corner stone was laid November 28, 1903, and the completed building opened to the public for distribution of books on the 30th of January, 1905. Its total capacity including the radial stacks and book shelving is 50,000 volumes A young men's debating club, school boys' literary club and public lectures held once a week in the auditorium, are educational features carried on in this branch

BOOK STACK AND SHELVING FOR LIBRARIES

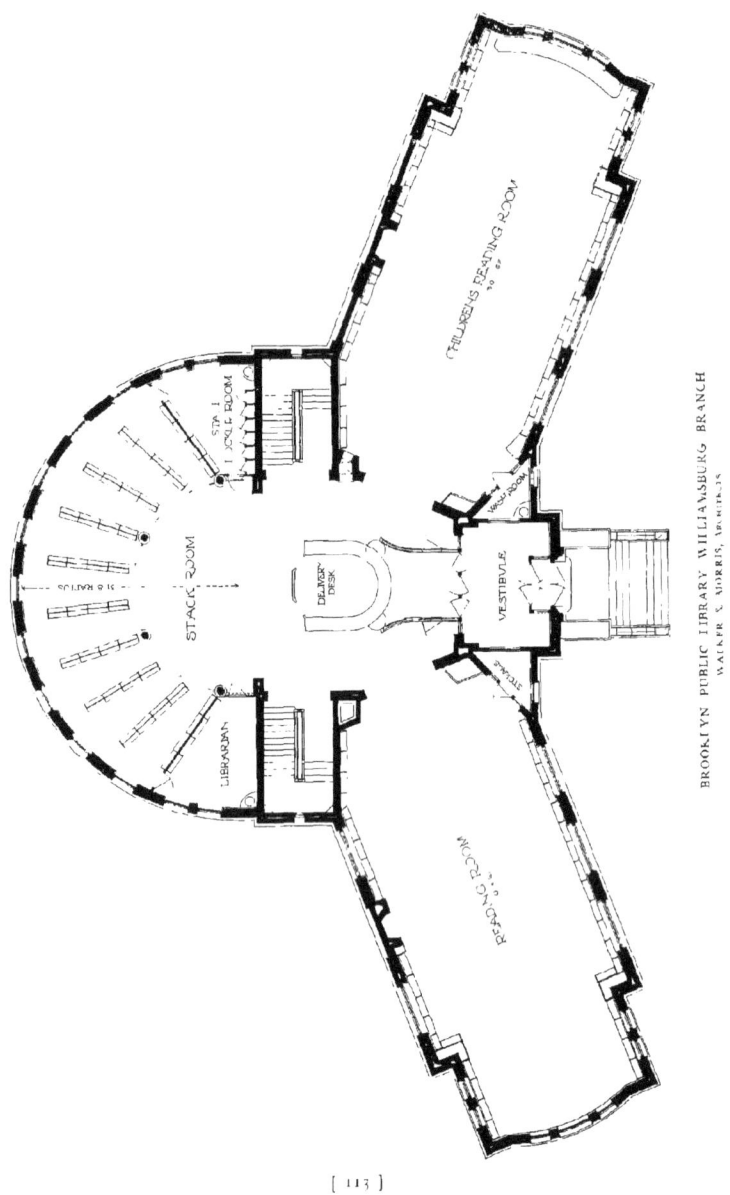

THE SNEAD AND COMPANY IRON WORKS

BROOKLYN PUBLIC LIBRARY, WILLIAMSBURG BRANCH
WALKER & MORRIS, Architects

BOOK STACK AND SHELVING FOR LIBRARIES

BROOKLYN PUBLIC LIBRARY, PACIFIC BRANCH
RAYMOND F ALMIRALL, Architect

THE SNEAD AND COMPANY IRON WORKS

BROOKLYN PUBLIC LIBRARY, PACIFIC BRANCH BROOKLYN, N. Y.

RAYMOND F ALMIRALL, Architect

THE Pacific Branch Library is situated at the corner of Fourth Avenue and 12th Street, Brooklyn. The exterior of brick and terra cotta is in good character and well denotes the purpose of the building

Entering through the vestibule and hall access to the rooms in the first and second stories can be had only through the stack and reading room, thereby causing all visitors to pass in full view of the delivery desk The radial stacks are grouped in pairs with wide aisles between the groups for the reception of reading tables in each of the two stack tiers The total capacity of the stacks is 30,000 volumes.

At either side of the hall and entered from the stack room are the reference room, staff and librarian's rooms

The front basement contains the machinery room, boiler room, work room and toilets At the rear and occupying the entire area under the stack room is a well lighted lecture hall with anteroom and janitor's room

A feature of this library is the children's room which occupies the entire second story over the stack and reading rooms It is fitted with tables, chairs, shelving and a fireplace At the front of the building in this story two study rooms each 20 feet 6 inches by 27 feet 3 inches are provided

BOOK STACK AND SHELVING FOR LIBRARIES

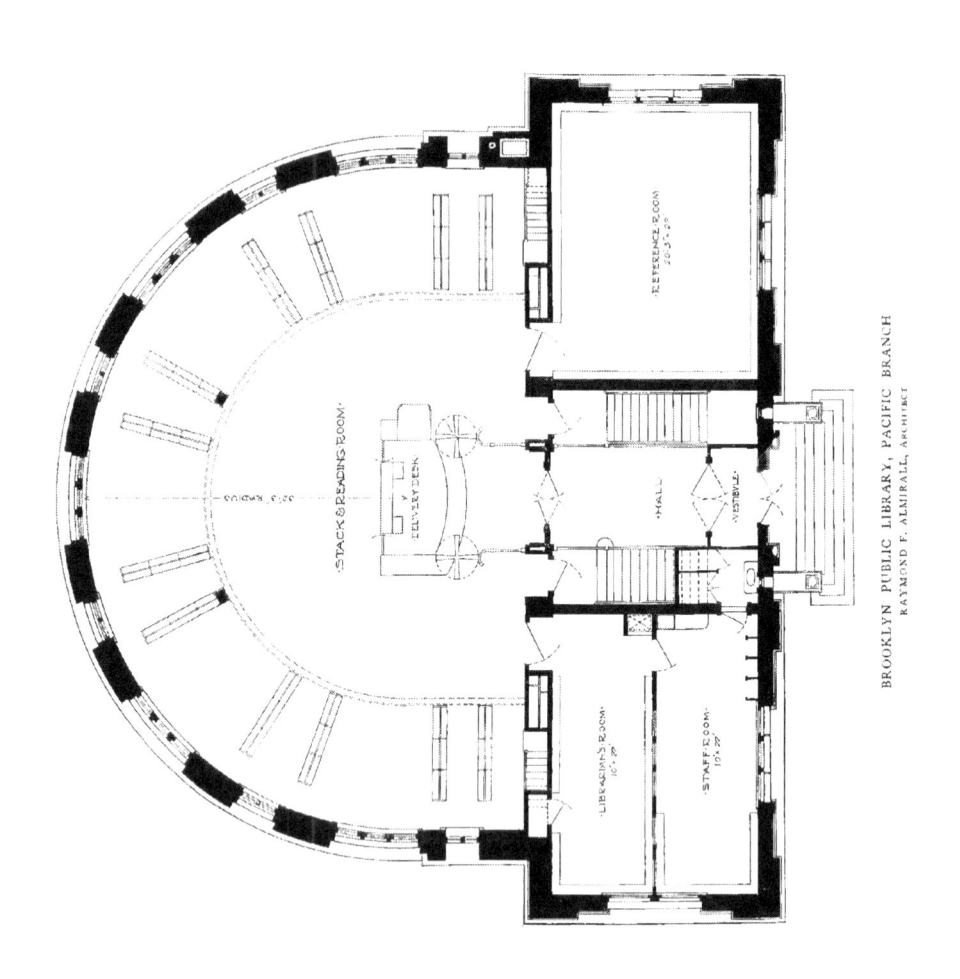

BROOKLYN PUBLIC LIBRARY, PACIFIC BRANCH
RAYMOND F. ALMIRALL, ARCHITECT

THE SNEAD AND COMPANY IRON WORKS

BROOKLYN PUBLIC LIBRARY, PACIFIC BRANCH
RAYMOND F. ALMIRALL, Architect

BOOK STACK AND SHELVING FOR LIBRARIES

BROOKLYN PUBLIC LIBRARY, CARROLL PARK BRANCH
WM. B. TUBBY & BRO., ARCHITECTS

THE SNEAD AND COMPANY IRON WORKS

BROOKLYN PUBLIC LIBRARY, CARROLL PARK BRANCH BROOKLYN, N Y.

WM B TUBBY & BRO, Architects

THE plan of this building is radically different from that of either branch library illustrated in the preceding pages but is admirably worked out and adapted to its site   The first story rooms have a ceiling about 21 feet high and are lighted through large windows extending nearly the full height, in addition to which ample skylights are placed over the reading room, children's room and the delivery desk The partitions between the front rooms in this story are only four feet high, enabling the attendants at the desk to command the entire floor

At the rear is the stack room 23 ft by 37 ft containing two stories of metal stacks with capacity of 29,000 volumes   The outer faces of these stacks have been provided with closed box ends to accommodate the electric conduits and switch boxes that control the lighting of the stack room

The other public rooms in this building are located in the basement   At the left under the reading room will be found two study rooms each about 12 ft 6 in by 16 ft 6 in and one study 23 ft by 33 ft At the right are the work room and staff room, each 17 ft by 23 ft 6 in , a room for the janitor and lavatories for the staff and for the public

In the center and rear basement directly under the stacks and delivery desk is a fine lecture room 36 ft 9 in by 45 ft fitted with a stage, well lighted and having a direct entrance from the street

A cellar has been excavated on the right hand side below the staff and work rooms and space provided here for the fan, boiler and coal rooms   The remaining area of the building has not been excavated below the basement floor

BOOK STACK AND SHELVING FOR LIBRARIES

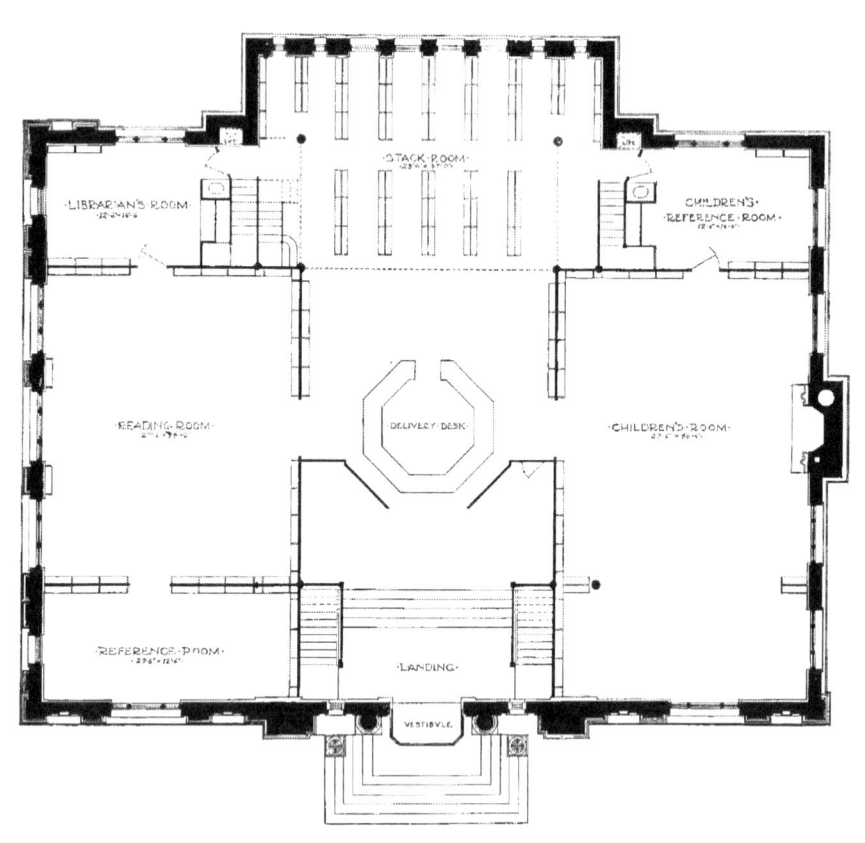

BROOKLYN PUBLIC LIBRARY, CARROLL PARK BRANCH
WM. B. TUBBY & BRO., Architects

THE SNEAD AND COMPANY IRON WORKS

BROOKLYN PUBLIC LIBRARY, CARROLL PARK BRANCH
WM. B. TUBBY & BRO., ARCHITECTS

BOOK STACK AND SHELVING FOR LIBRARIES

FLOWER MEMORIAL LIBRARY, WATERTOWN, N. Y.
ORCHARD, LANSING & JORALEMON, ARCHITECTS
I. & R. LAMB, INTERIOR DECORATORS

THE SNEAD AND COMPANY IRON WORKS

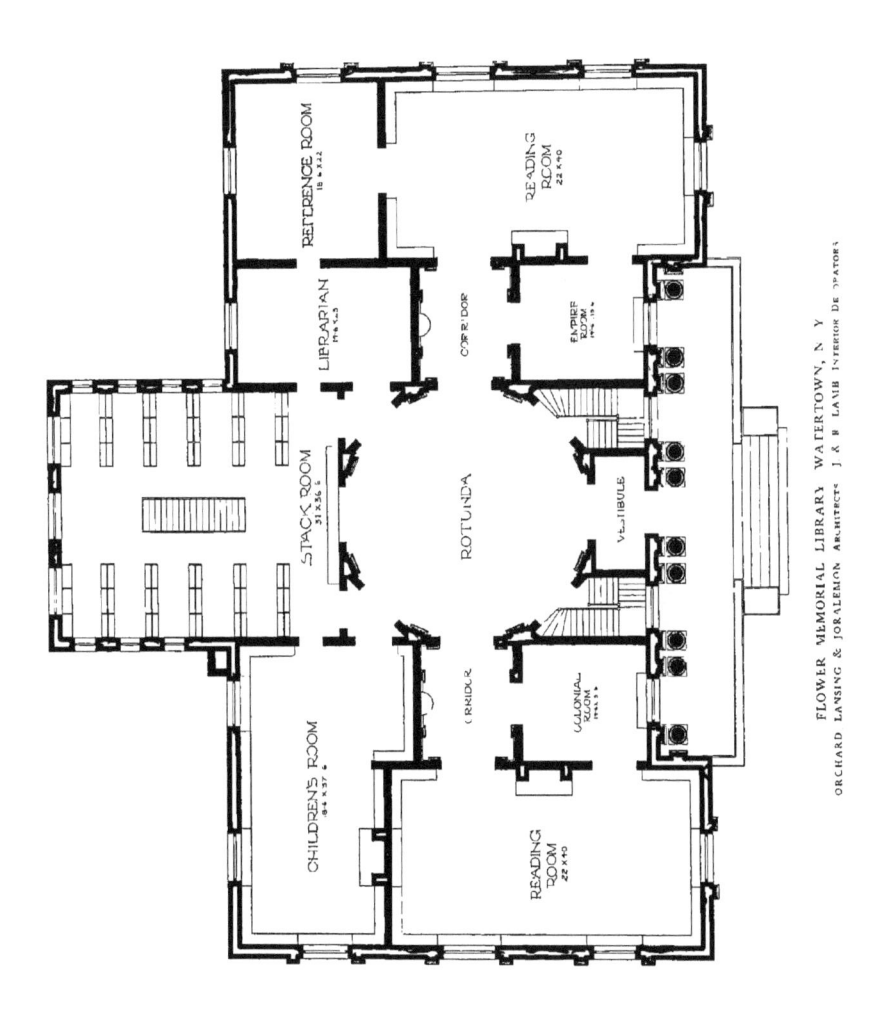

BOOK STACK AND SHELVING FOR LIBRARIES

BOOK STACKS IN FIRST STORY

BOOK STACKS IN BASEMENT

FLOWER MEMORIAL LIBRARY, WATERTOWN, N. Y.
ORCHARD, LANSING & JORALEMON, ARCHITECTS
J. & R. LAMB, INTERIOR DECORATORS

THE SNEAD AND COMPANY IRON WORKS

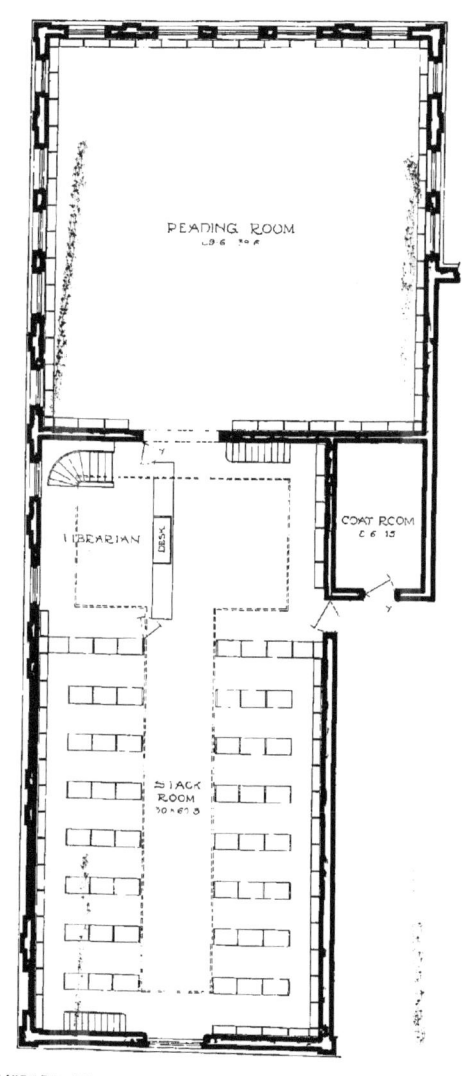

LIBRARY OF THEOLOGICAL SEMINARY, ROCHESTER, N. Y.
J. FOSTER WARNER ARCHITECT

BOOK STACK AND SHELVING FOR LIBRARIES

ROCHESTER THEOLOGICAL SEMINARY, ROCHESTER, N. Y.
J. FOSTER WARNER, ARCHITECT

THE SNEAD AND COMPANY IRON WORKS

WASHINGTON PUBLIC LIBRARY, WASHINGTON, D. C.
ALBERT RANDOLPH ROSS, Architect

BOOK STACK AND SHELVING FOR LIBRARIES

WASHINGTON PUBLIC LIBRARY, WASHINGTON, D. C.
ALBERT RANDOLPH ROSS, ARCHITECT

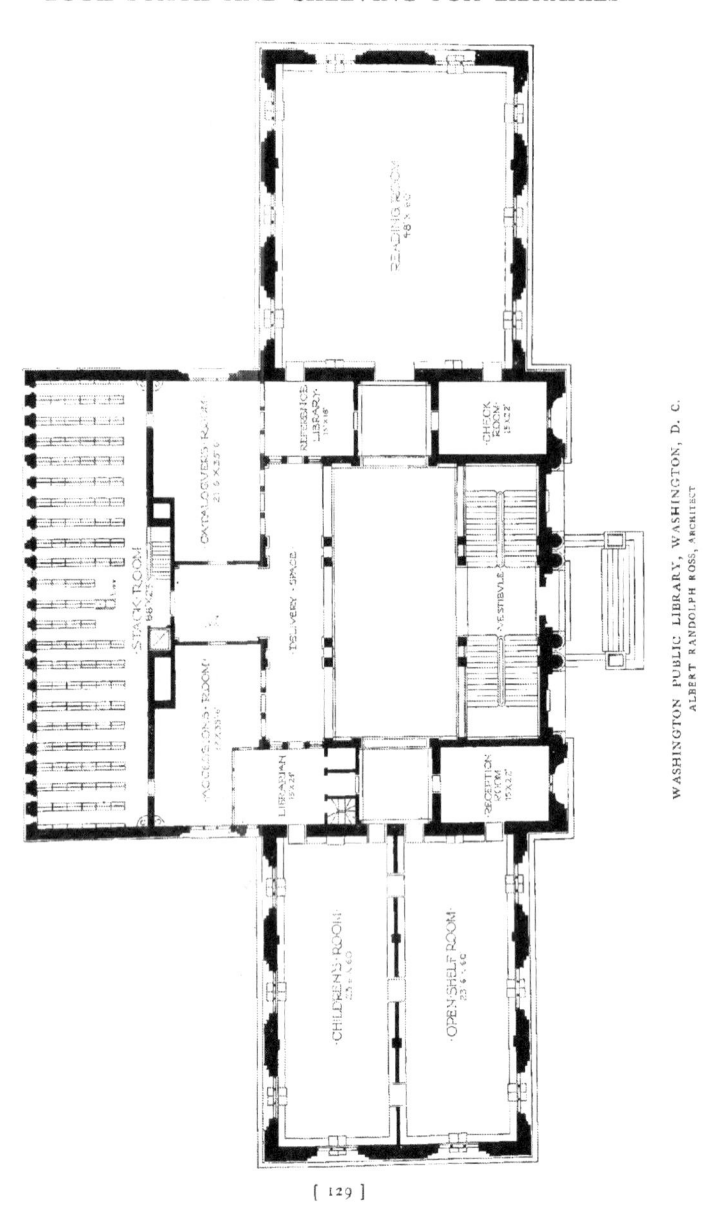

THE SNEAD AND COMPANY IRON WORKS

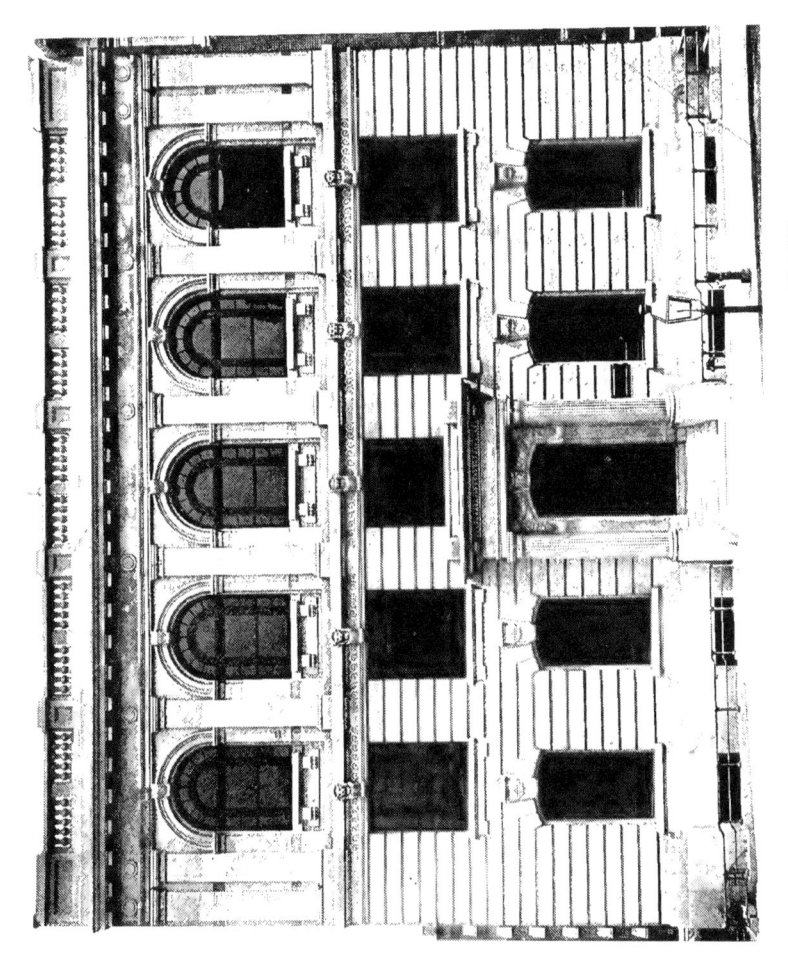

JEWISH THEOLOGICAL SEMINARY OF AMERICA, NEW YORK CITY
ARNOLD W. BRUNNER, ARCHITECT

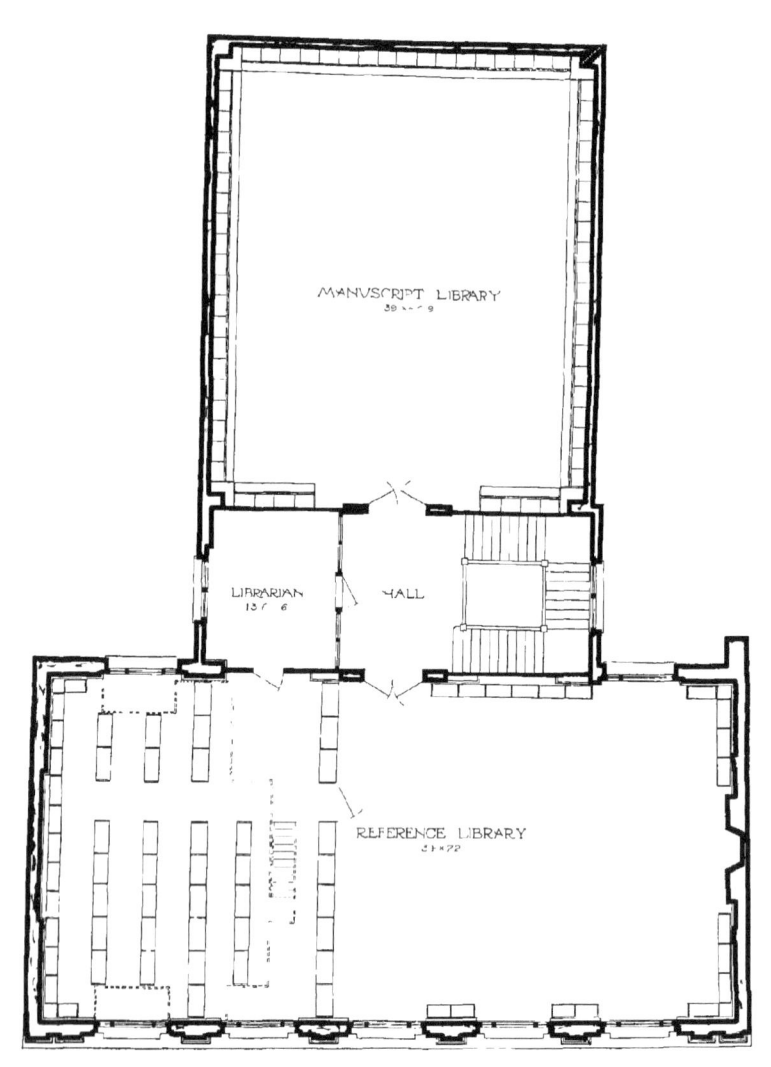

BOOK STACK AND SHELVING FOR LIBRARIES

LIBRARY JEWISH THEOLOGICAL SEMINARY OF AMERICA, NEW YORK CITY
ARNOLD W. BRUNNER, ARCHITECT

THE SNEAD AND COMPANY IRON WORKS

MANUSCRIPT LIBRARY, JEWISH THEOLOGICAL SEMINARY OF AMERICA, NEW YORK CITY

ARNOLD W BRUNNER, Architect

THE library rooms of the seminary are located in the third story   In the reference library the books are shelved in the standard open stacks, but the rare and valuable possessions of the manuscript library are placed under lock and key in specially constructed cases provided with glass doors   The shelves in these cases are of the skeleton steel type and adjustable, being 24 inches deep in the lower compartments and 15 inches deep above

The manuscript library room is fireproof, having no windows, and is lighted from above   It contains more than 12,000 volumes, constituting the largest collection of rare Hebraica in the United States and the fourth largest in the world

BOOK STACK AND SHELVING FOR LIBRARIES

MANUSCRIPT LIBRARY, JEWISH THEOLOGICAL SEMINARY OF AMERICA, NEW YORK CITY
ARNOLD W. BRUNNER, ARCHITECT

THE SNEAD AND COMPANY IRON WORKS

TORONTO PUBLIC REFERENCE LIBRARY, TORONTO, ONT.
WICKSON & GREGG AND A. H. CHAPMAN, ARCHITECTS

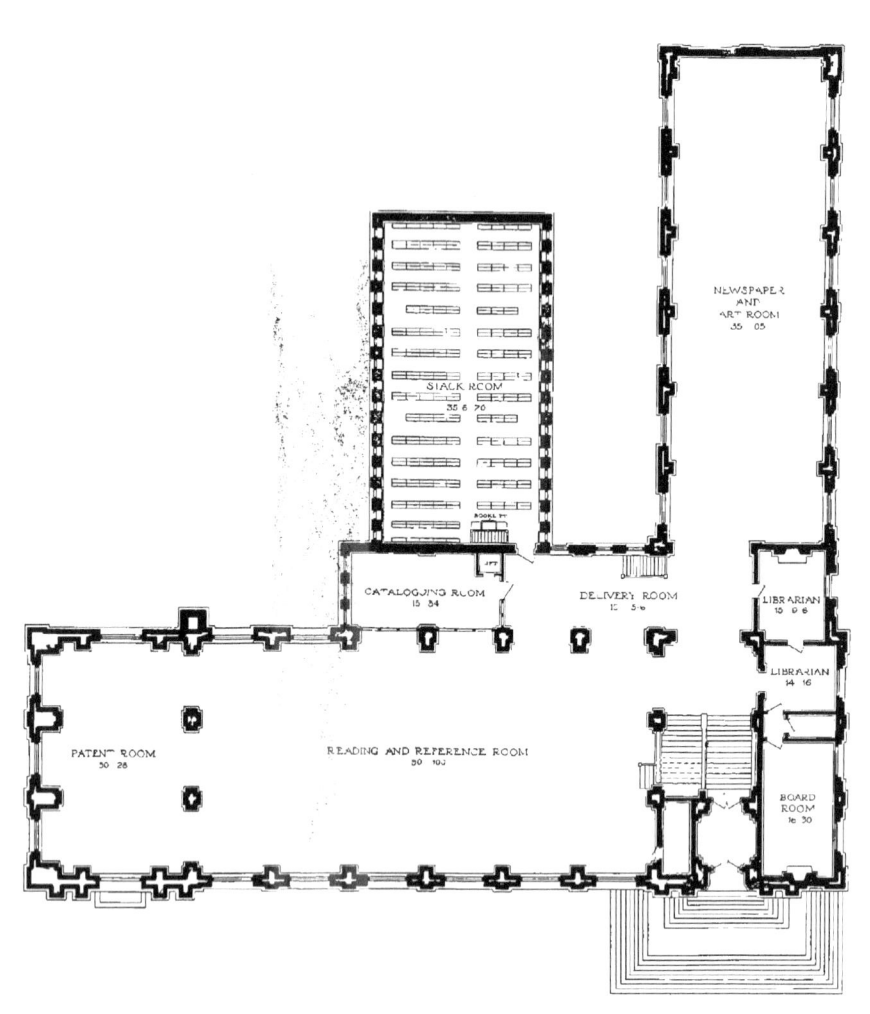

BOOK STACK AND SHELVING FOR LIBRARIES

TORONTO PUBLIC REFERENCE LIBRARY, TORONTO, ONT.
WICKSON & GREGG AND A. H. CHAPMAN, ARCHITECTS

THE SNEAD AND COMPANY IRON WORKS

FALL RIVER PUBLIC LIBRARY, FALL RIVER, MASS.
CRAM, GOODHUE & FERGUSON, ARCHITECTS

BOOK STACK AND SHELVING FOR LIBRARIES

FALL RIVER PUBLIC LIBRARY, FALL RIVER, MASS
CRAM, GOODHUE & FERGUSON, ARCHITECTS

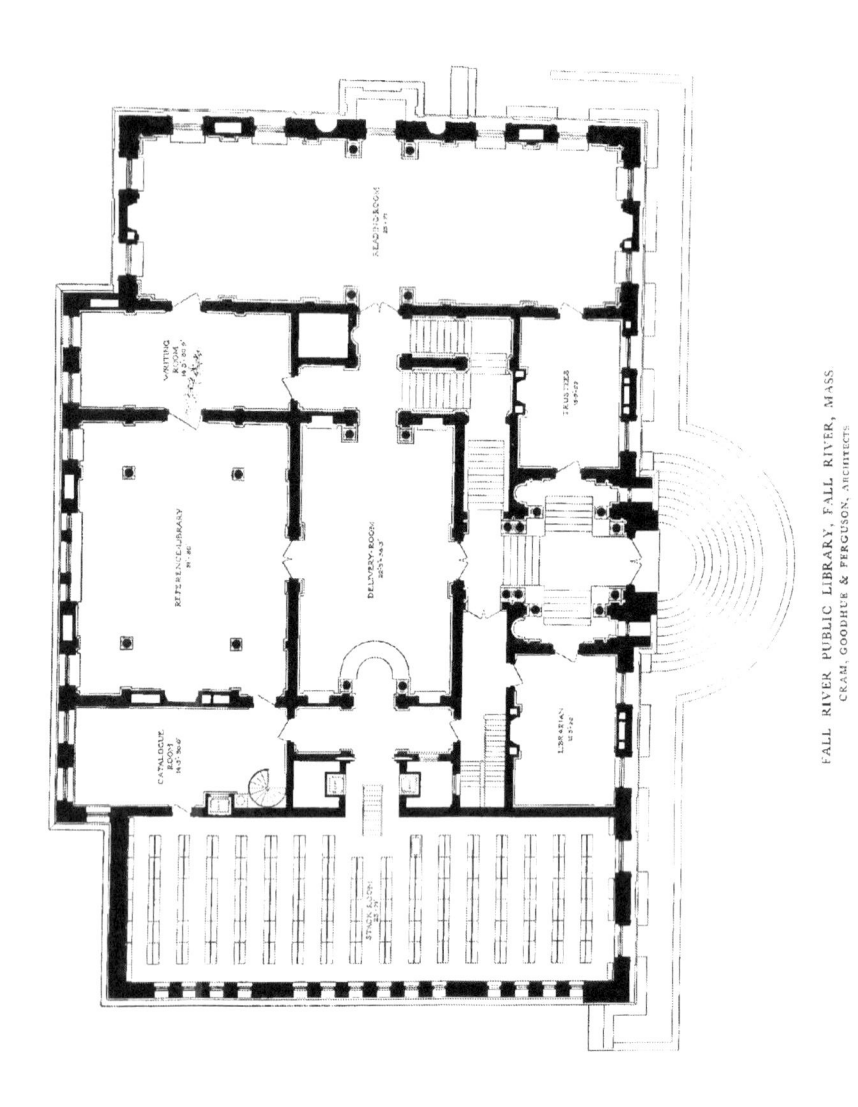

THE SNEAD AND COMPANY IRON WORKS

FALL RIVER PUBLIC LIBRARY, FALL RIVER, MASS
CRAM, GOODHUE & FERGUSON, Architects

BOOK STACK AND SHELVING FOR LIBRARIES

CONVERSE MEMORIAL LIBRARY, MALDEN, MASS.
SHEPLEY, RUTAN & COOLIDGE, Architects

THE SNEAD AND COMPANY IRON WORKS

STATE LIBRARY, CONCORD, N. H.
A. P. CUTTING, Architect

BOOK STACK AND SHELVING FOR LIBRARIES

STATE LIBRARY, CONCORD, N. H.
(BOOKSTACKS IN ALCOVES)
A. P. CUTTING, ARCHITECT

THE SNEAD AND COMPANY IRON WORKS

MASONIC LIBRARY, BOSTON, MASS
LORING & PHIPPS, Architects

BOOK STACK AND SHELVING FOR LIBRARIES

CARNEGIE PUBLIC LIBRARY, SYRACUSE, N. Y.
JAMES A. RANDALL, ARCHITECT

THE SNEAD AND COMPANY IRON WORKS

STATE NORMAL SCHOOL, TERRE HAUTE, IND.
W. L. B. JENNEY AND W. H. FLOYD, Architects

BOOK STACK AND SHELVING FOR LIBRARIES

STATE NORMAL SCHOOL, TERRE HAUTE, IND.
W. L. B. JENNEY AND W. H. FLOYD, ARCHITECTS

THE SNEAD AND COMPANY IRON WORKS

LIBRARY OF THE NEW YORK LAW ASSOCIATION, POST-OFFICE BUILDING, NEW YORK CITY

BOOK STACK AND SHELVING FOR LIBRARIES

PARLIAMENTARY LIBRARY, WELLINGTON, NEW ZEALAND
JOHN CAMPBELL, GOVERNMENT ARCHITECT

THE SNEAD AND COMPANY IRON WORKS

STATE AGRICULTURAL COLLEGE, MANHATTAN, KAN.
SEYMOUR DAVIS, Architect

BOOK STACK AND SHELVING FOR LIBRARIES

MAINE HISTORICAL SOCIETY, PORTLAND, ME.
F. H. FASSETT, ARCHITECT

THE SNEAD AND COMPANY IRON WORKS

LELAND STANFORD, Jr., UNIVERSITY LIBRARY STANFORD UNIVERSITY, CAL.
(BOOK STACKS PREPARED TO RECEIVE ADDITIONAL TIER)
CHAS. EDWARD HODGES, ARCHITECT

BOOK STACK AND SHELVING FOR LIBRARIES

AMERICAN SOCIETY FOR PREVENTION OF CRUELTY TO ANIMALS, NEW YORK CITY
RENWICK, ASPINWALL & OWEN, ARCHITECTS

THE SNEAD AND COMPANY IRON WORKS

BLACKSTONE MEMORIAL LIBRARY, BRANFORD, CONN.
S. S. BEMAN, Architect

BLACKSTONE MEMORIAL LIBRARY, BRANFORD, CONN
S. S. BEMAN, ARCHITECT

THE SNEAD AND COMPANY IRON WORKS

NEWSPAPER FILE

IT is merely a round stick of wood 1 inch in diameter with rounded ends, 34 inches long, smooth all over and handsomely finished and polished

Each newspaper is held rigidly in a longitudinal groove in the stick by a thin steel rod confined at the ends by thin brass rings

The papers are quickly released and inserted, to the number of seven, more or less as desired, say a week's issue

Papers are held firmly and evenly as in a binder, without punching, cutting or pinching of the paper

Papers are always in regular order by date and page, like a book

The stick has no projection or roughness and is all as smooth as a walking stick, whether filled with papers or empty

There is nothing about the file to get out of order, while it is as simple as a broom stick, but equally as tough and durable

Hundreds of them have been for years in most satisfactory use in the public reading rooms of the Library of Congress

Manufactured and For Sale by

THE SNEAD AND COMPANY IRON WORKS
JERSEY CITY, N J

BOOK STACK AND SHELVING FOR LIBRARIES

NEWSPAPER FILE

THE SNEAD AND COMPANY IRON WORKS

THE SNEAD AND COMPANY IRON WORKS
(Incorporated)
JERSEY CITY, N J

ARCHITECTURAL IRON AND BRONZE WORK FOR BUILDINGS
AND
BOOK STACKS FOR LIBRARIES

FINE CASTINGS IN IRON, BRONZE, BRASS AND ALUMINUM
HIGH-CLASS HAND FORGED WROUGHT IRON WORK

STAIRWAYS	RAILINGS
GRILLES	MARQUEES
GATES	ELEVATOR CABS
LANTERNS	ELEVATOR SCREENS
STORE FRONTS AND WINDOWS	

This company has been in successful operation for over 50 years and almost every large city in the country has important examples of its manufacture

BOOK STACK AND SHELVING FOR LIBRARIES

VESTIBULE AT RESIDENCE OF CORNELIUS
VANDERBILT, NEW YORK CITY
DELANO & ALDRICH, Architects

STAIRWAY IN MARSHALL FIELD BUILDING
CHICAGO, ILL.

CAST IRON BALCONY RAILING, BOSTON PUBLIC LIBRARY
McKIM, MEAD & WHITE, Architects

THE SNEAD AND COMPANY IRON WORKS

INDEX

ARCHITECTS	PAGE
Allen & Collens,	20
Raymond F Almirall,	115
S S Beman,	152
Arnold W Brunner,	130
John Campbell,	147
Carrère & Hastings,	83
Clarke & Russell,	19
Cope & Stewardson,	20
Cram, Goodhue & Ferguson,	136
A P Cutting,	140
Seymour Davis,	148
Frank Miles Day & Bro,	20
C L W Eidlitz,	18
F H Fassett,	17-149
H M Francis,	19
Furness & Evans,	19
Raleigh C Gildersleeve,	18
Chas C Haight,	18
Chas Edw Hodges,	150
Howe, Hoit & Cutler,	19
W L B Jenney & W H Floyd,	144
Loring & Phipps,	142
McKim, Mead & White,	20
Orchard, Lansing & Joralemon,	123
Parish & Schroeder,	17
Perkins & Betton,	19
Pilcher & Tachau,	99
W M Poindexter,	18
James A Randall,	143
Rankin, Kellogg & Crane,	20
Renwick, Aspinwall & Owen,	19-151
Jas Gamble Rogers & Chas A Phillips,	103
Albert Randolph Ross,	128
Rotch & Tilden,	19
Shepley, Rutan & Coolidge,	139
Smithmeyer & Pelz and Edward P Casey,	71
Supervising Architect, Treasury Department,	18-146
Wm B Tubby & Bro,	119
Walker & Morris,	111
J Foster Warner,	126
Watson & Huckel,	107
Wickson & Gregg, and A H Chapman,	134
Wilson, Harris & Richards,	20
Winslow & Bigelow,	18
Academy of Natural Sciences, Philadelphia, Pa,	20
Accessories,	58
Adjustable Steel Shelf,	6-7
Adjustable Steel Shelf,	9-11
Air cleaning or dusting,	11
American Philosophical Society, Philadelphia, Pa,	20
American Society of Civil Engineers, New York City,	18
American Society for Prevention of Cruelty to Animals, New York City Interior view of library,	151
Appellate Court Library, Mt Vernon, Ill,	19
Architectural Iron and Bronze,	156-157
Army War College, Washington, D C,	20
Automatic book lift,	70

	PAGE
Back stop for books,	58-59
Benedict College Library, Columbia, S C,	20
Blackstone Memorial Library, Branford, Conn	
Exterior view,	152
Interior, showing stacks,	153
Book carrier,	10
Book carrier,	70
Book lift,	70
Bookstack,	46-47
Book support,	9-12
Book support,	28-29
Book support,	48-49
Book support,	58-59
Bracket shelf,	60-61-63
Bracket stack, cast iron,	60-61-62-64
Bracket stack, steel,	60-63-64
Bronze work,	156
Brooklyn Public Library, Brooklyn, N Y	
Williamsburg Branch,	111
Pacific Branch,	115
Carroll Park Branch,	119
Brush for perforated shelf,	59
Canton Public Library, Canton, Mass,	18
Capacity of shelving,	65
Card frame,	42-52
Card holder, hanging,	58-59
Carrier for books,	10-70
Carroll Park Branch Library, Brooklyn, N Y	
Exterior view,	119
Description of building,	120
First floor plan,	121
Interior, showing stacks,	122
Cast iron bracket stack,	60-61-62
Cast iron horns,	26-27
Cast iron horns,	36-37
Cast iron horns,	40-41
Cast iron, its uses,	26
Cast iron shelf supports, Government tests,	52
Circulating library,	65
Closed end for bracket stack,	60-64
College of Physicians, Philadelphia, Pa,	20
Construction of the bookstack,	7
Converse Memorial Library, Malden, Mass	
Interior of stack room,	139
Deck plan,	30-31
Deck slit,	30-31
Deck slit,	6-8-14
Department of Agriculture, Washington, D C,	20
Depth of shelf,	65
Diagonal braces,	54-55
Diaphragm,	8
Diaphragm,	38-39
Diaphragm,	52
Disinfecting bookstacks,	46
Double-faced range,	52-53
Double-faced range,	54-55
Duct for electric wires,	32-33

[158]

BOOK STACK AND SHELVING FOR LIBRARIES

INDEX — Continued

	PAGE
Duct for electric wires,	35
Duct for electric wires,	69
Dust brush for perforated shelf,	59
Dusting,	11
Electric book lift,	70
Electric lighting,	6
Electric lighting,	32
Electric lighting,	69
Electric wire ducts,	32-33
Electric wire ducts,	35
Electric wire ducts,	69
Elevator and stairs,	10
Evanston Public Library, Evanston, Ill.	
Exterior view,	103
Description of building,	104
First floor plan,	105
Interior showing stacks,	106
Exeter Public Library, Exeter, N. H.,	19
Fall River Public Library, Fall River, Mass.	
Exterior view,	136
First floor plan	137
Interior of Delivery Hall,	138
Finish of stack and shelf,	52
Fletcher Library, Westford, Mass.	19
Flower Memorial Library, Watertown, N. Y.	
Exterior view,	123
First floor plan	124
Interiors of stack rooms,	125
General considerations,	11
General considerations,	15
General principles of bookstacks and shelving,	6
General Theological Seminary, New York City,	18
Glass flooring,	6
Glass flooring,	38-39
Glass flooring,	67
Hand power book lift,	70
Hanging card frame,	59
Heating and ventilation,	10
History of bookstacks	4
Hyde Park Library, Hyde Park, Mass.,	19
Indiana State Normal School, Terre Haute, Ind.	
Interior view, showing wall stacks,	144
Interior view, showing two-tier stack,	145
Isometric drawing of 20-inch stack	39
Isometric drawing of 16-inch stack	41
Jewish Theological Seminary of America, New York City	
Exterior view,	130
Plan of library floor,	131
Description of Manuscript Library,	132
Interior view of Manuscript Library,	133
Kansas State Agricultural College, Manhattan, Kan.	
Interior view of library,	148
Krauth Memorial Library, Mt. Airy, Pa.	
Exterior view,	107
Description of building,	108
First floor plan	109
Interior of stack room,	110
Label holder,	10

	PAGE
Label holder,	48-49
Label holder,	59
Law Library,	65
Ledge,	27
Ledge,	29
Ledge,	53
Leland Stanford, Jr., University Library, Stanford University, California	
Interior of stack room,	150
Library of Congress, Washington, D. C.	
Plan of the north stack,	23
Longitudinal section of the north stack,	24
Cross section of the north stack,	25
Description of building,	72
Exterior,	74
First floor plan,	75
Second floor plan,	76
Longitudinal section,	77
Main Reading Room,	78
View at stairway in the North Stack,	79
Exterior of the North Stack,	80
Floor in the North Stack,	81
Perspective between decks,	45
Libraries using the Green system of bookstack and shelving,	17
Lift for books,	70
Lighting of stacks,	8
Lighting of stacks	32-33
Lighting of stacks,	69
Littleton Public Library, Littleton, Mass.,	19
Loads of stacks and floors,	67-68
Louisville Free Public Library, Louisville, Ky.	
Exterior view	99
Description of building,	100
First floor plan,	101
Interior of stack room,	102
Lutheran Theological Seminary, Mt. Airy, Pa.,	107
Maine Historical Society, Portland, Me.	
Interior view, showing stacks,	149
Malden Public Library, Malden, Mass.	
Interior of stack room,	139
Marble flooring,	6
Marble flooring,	8
Marble flooring,	38-39
Marble flooring,	68
Masonic Library, Boston, Mass.	
Interior view,	142
New Hampshire State Library, Concord, N. H.	
Exterior view,	140
Interior view,	141
Newspaper file,	154-155
New York Genealogical and Biographical Society, New York City,	20
New York Law Association Library, New York City	
Interior view,	146
New York Public Library, New York City	
Range front and shelf support,	42-43
Description of building,	84
Plaster model of building,	86

[159]

THE SNEAD AND COMPANY IRON WORKS

INDEX — Continued

	Page		Page
New York Public Library, New York City		Shelf supports for 8-inch shelf,	36-37
Front elevation,	87	Shelf supports for 8-inch shelf,	40-41
Rear elevation,	88	Shelf supports for cast iron bracket stack,	60-61
First floor plan,	89	Shelf supports for steel bracket stack,	60-63
Second floor plan,	90	Single faced range,	56-57
Third floor plan,	91	Skeleton steel shelf,	8-9
Stack frame in process of erection,	92	Skeleton steel shelf,	28-29
Stack frame supporting Reading Room floor	93	Skeleton steel shelf,	48-49
First tier of stack,	94	Small libraries	15
Intermediate tier of stack	95	Stack for 10-inch shelf,	39
Model of stack,	96	Stack for 8-inch shelf,	41
Original design of bookstack,	4	Stack loads,	67-68
Pacific Branch Library, Brooklyn, N Y		Stack weights,	66
Exterior view,	115	Stairs,	10
Description of building	116	Standard dimensions of shelves,	7
First floor plan,	117	Standard tier height	6-26
Interior, showing stacks,	118	Steel bracket stack,	60-63-64
Parliamentary Library, Wellington, New Zealand		Steel columns,	28-29
Interior view	147	Steel columns,	42-43
Perfect bookstack,	5	Steel horns	36-37
Perspective of stack between decks,	44-45	Steel horns	38-39
Perspective view of stack,	46-47	Strength of cast-iron shelf supports,	52
Pilaster end for bracket stack,	60-64	Strength of skeleton steel shelf,	48
Plan of deck and ranges,	30-31	Sydney Public Library, Sydney, N S W,	20
Portable ledge,	14	Syracuse Public Library, Syracuse, N Y	
Portable ledge,	27-29	Interior view, showing stacks,	143
Portland Public Library, Portland, Me ,	17	Tests of cast-iron shelf supports,	52
Public Library,	65	Test of skeleton steel shelf	48
Range for 10-inch shelves,	52-53	Toronto Public Reference Library, Toronto, Ontario	
Range for 10-inch shelves,	54-55	Exterior view,	134
Range for 10-inch shelves,	56-57	Main floor plan,	135
Range front for 10-inch shelf,	26-27	Union Theological Seminary, New York City,	20
Range front for 10-inch shelf,	32-33	University of Pennsylvania Library, Philadelphia, Pa ,	19
Range front for 9-inch shelf,	42-43	United States Naval Home, Philadelphia, Pa ,	20
Range front for 8-inch shelf,	34-35	Ventilation	10
Reference library,	65	Virginia State Library, Richmond, Va ,	18
Requisites of a library bookstack,	3	Wall range,	56-57
Ridgefield Memorial Library, Ridgefield, Conn ,	18	Washington Public Library, Washington, D C	
Rochester Theological Seminary, Rochester, N Y		Exterior view,	128
First floor plan of library,	126	First floor plan,	129
Interior of stack room	127	Weight of shelf,	48
Roller shelf,	50-51	Weights of stacks and floors,	66
School of Mines and Metallurgy, Rolla, Mo ,	19	Western College for Women, Oxford, O ,	19
Scientific library	65	Wheeling Public Library Wheeling, W Va ,	19
Shelf brush,	59	Williamsburg Branch Library, Brooklyn, N Y	
Shelf supports,	8	Exterior view,	111
Shelf supports,	39-41	Description of building,	112
Shelf supports and shelves,	8	First floor plan,	113
Shelf supports for 10-inch shelf,	26-27	Interior, showing stacks,	114
Shelf supports for 10-inch shelf,	36-37	Window seat,	30-31
Shelf supports for 10-inch shelf,	38-39	Window seat,	44-45
Shelf supports for 9-inch shelf,	42-43	Y M C A Library, New York City	17

BOOK STACK AND SHELVING FOR LIBRARIES

SUPPLEMENT

THE SNEAD AND COMPANY IRON WORKS

IMPORTANT CONTRACTS RECEIVED IN 1908, 1909, AND 1910

AMERICAN GEOGRAPHICAL SOCIETY
NEW YORK CITY
CHARLES P HUNTINGTON, Architect

BOSTON ATHENÆUM
BOSTON, MASS
J R WORCESTER & CO, Engineers

BROOKLINE PUBLIC LIBRARY
BROOKLINE, MASS
R CLIPSTON STURGIS, Architect

COAST ARTILLERY SCHOOL LIBRARY
FORT MONROE, VA
FRANCIS B WHEATON, Architect

DENVER PUBLIC LIBRARY
DENVER, COL
ALBERT RANDOLPH ROSS, Architect

GRATZ COLLEGE LIBRARY
PHILADELPHIA, PA
PILCHER & TACHAU, Architects

HARPER MEMORIAL LIBRARY
UNIVERSITY OF CHICAGO
SHEPLEY, RUTAN & COOLIDGE, Architects

HISPANIC SOCIETY OF AMERICA
NEW YORK CITY
CHARLES P HUNTINGTON, Architect

KENT HALL, COLUMBIA UNIVERSITY
NEW YORK CITY
McKIM, MEAD & WHITE, Architects

McGILL UNIVERSITY MEDICAL LIBRARY
MONTREAL, CANADA
DAVID R BROWN and HUGH VALLANCE, Architects

MEDICAL AND CHIRURGICAL FACULTY OF MARYLAND
BALTIMORE, MD
ELLICOTT & EMMART, Architects

BOOK STACK AND SHELVING FOR LIBRARIES

OTTAWA PUBLIC LIBRARY
OTTAWA, CANADA
EDGAR L HORWOOD, Architect

STATE UNIVERSITY OF IOWA LAW LIBRARY
IOWA CITY, IA
PROUDFOOT & BIRD, Architects

TEXAS STATE LIBRARY
AUSTIN, TEX
E E MYERS, Architect

UNIVERSITY OF ILLINOIS
URBANA, ILL
JAMES M WHITE, Architect

MERCANTILE LIBRARY
ST LOUIS, MO
MAURAN & RUSSELL, Architects

VICTORIA COLLEGE LIBRARY
TORONTO, ONTARIO
SPROATT & ROLPH, Architects

ANDOVER THEOLOGICAL SEMINARY
CAMBRIDGE, MASS
ALLEN & COLLENS, Architects

CORNELL UNIVERSITY LAW LIBRARY
ITHACA, N Y
WILLIAM H MILLER, Architect

COLUMBIA UNIVERSITY LIBRARY
NEW YORK CITY
McKIM, MEAD & WHITE, Architects

COBURN FREE LIBRARY
OWEGO, N Y
H SUMNER GARDNER, Architect

ST CHARLES BORROMEO SEMINARY
OVERBROOK, PA
WILSON, HARRIS & RICHARDS, Architects

WISCONSIN STATE CAPITOL
MADISON, WIS
GEORGE B POST & SONS, Architects

UNIVERSITY OF MICHIGAN LIBRARY
ANN ARBOR, MICH
ALBERT KAHN, Architect

THE SNEAD AND COMPANY IRON WORKS

TECHNICAL SCIENCE READING ROOM, NEW YORK PUBLIC LIBRARY
CARRÈRE & HASTINGS, Architects

BOOK STACK AND SHELVING FOR LIBRARIES

NEWSPAPER SECTION, SOUTHEAST COURT BOOK STACK, LIBRARY OF CONGRESS, WASHINGTON, D. C.

THE SNEAD AND COMPANY IRON WORKS

VIEW FROM DELIVERY ROOM, DENVER PUBLIC LIBRARY
ALBERT RANDOLPH ROSS, Architect

BOOK STACK AND SHELVING FOR LIBRARIES

UPPER TIERS, DENVER PUBLIC LIBRARY
ALBERT RANDOLPH ROSS, Architect

CPSIA information can be obtained
at www.ICGtesting.com
Printed in the USA
BVHW042257171221
624352BV00003B/90